CARDIFF
& THE VALE IN THE
FIRST WORLD WAR

PHIL CARRADICE

AMBERLEY

First published 2014

Amberley Publishing
The Hill, Stroud
Gloucestershire, GL5 4EP

www.amberley-books.com

British Library Cataloguing in Publication Data.
A catalogue record for this book is available from the British Library.

ISBN 978 1 4456 1751 0 (paperback)
ISBN 978 1 4456 1758 9 (ebook)

Typeset in 10pt on 12pt Minion Pro.
Typesetting and Origination by Amberley Publishing.
Printed in the UK.

CARDIFF
& THE VALE IN THE
FIRST WORLD WAR

"ANIBYNIAETH
SYDD YN GALW
AM EI
DEWRAF DYN"

Contents

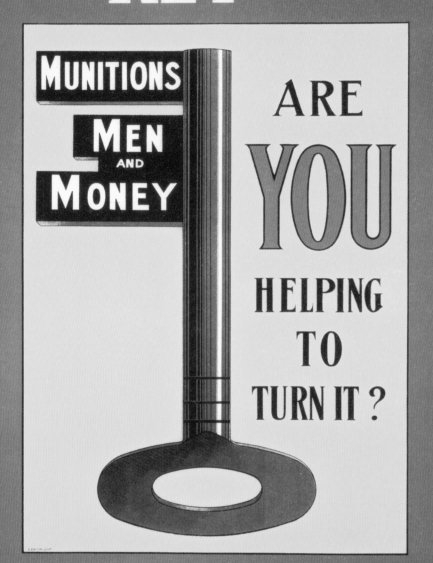

1

The Background

By the summer of 1914 the main ports of south-east Wales – Cardiff, Penarth and Barry – had become three of the richest and most economically viable trading centres in the world. It was a position and a wealth that was based upon one commodity – coal, the black gold of the Rhondda and Rhymney valleys.

The success of the ports was quite an achievement, considering that in the middle years of the nineteenth century Penarth and Barry were little more than tiny hamlets and Cardiff was still in the first throes of industrial growth. However, by the outbreak of the First World War they had achieved pre-eminence, and the way that they responded to this conflict – its outbreak, its continuation and its conclusion – is both illuminating and interesting.

In one respect the location of the three ports was a major factor in their success, each of them sitting at the seaward end of rich coal valleys, poised like nails on the ends of long thin fingers. The Glamorganshire Canal that first linked Cardiff to the coal mines of the interior quickly gave way to the railway system, and by the end of the century the people of Cardiff, Penarth and Barry were as used to the clanking of goods wagons as they were to the screaming of ships' sirens and hooters.

Yet, right from the beginning, the three ports were always something of an anomaly. The Vale of Glamorgan was one of the most beautiful and rural parts of Wales. Flat, rolling countryside that was ideal for dairy and arable farming did not lie easily with heavy industry and shipping. Nevertheless in the nineteenth and early twentieth centuries lie easily it did.

That's not all. It remains fascinating that, in addition to shipping and farming, all three towns, to a lesser or greater degree, soon developed a tourist industry, so miners and steelworkers from the hinterland – and, of course, visitors from across Offa's Dyke – could relax and enjoy amenities like a pleasure pier, paddle-steamer cruises on the Bristol Channel and exciting rides at a modern funfair.

The coming of war in 1914 brought misery and heartache to many of the people in the three towns – and to the villages of the Vale – and the proportion of men who died in the trenches and on the ships of the Royal Navy was probably as high there as in any other part of Wales. However, it also brought, for the shipowners and industrialists in particular, the opportunity for further growth and the accumulation of even more wealth.

It is this combination of 'good' and 'bad' that makes any study of the Vale of Glamorgan – and particularly of Cardiff, Penarth and Barry – in the First World War so fascinating.

BUCKINGHAM PALACE.

I join with my grateful people
in sending you this memorial
of a brave life given for others
in the Great War.

George R.I.

Nearly one million British men, women and children died in the First World War, and the Vale towns and villages paid a heavy price for their involvement. For many of the bereaved families, a few medals and a message from the king were scant consolation.

However, to truly understand the responses of the people in those communities to the conflict of 1914–18, one that suddenly erupted and threatened to overwhelm everyone, it is necessary to go back to the beginning and see how each town developed and grew over the years.

*

Cardiff was the first of the towns to be developed. There had been a settlement in the area since pre-Roman times, the Celtic tribe of the Silures laying claim to the territory. Then came the Romans and, after them, the Normans.

In 1081 the Normans built a castle keep within the walls of the old Roman fort and, gradually, a small town grew up in its shadow. In the Middle Ages the place had a population of nearly 2,000 and was a busy port, ships coming up the River Taff to load and unload at wharves close to the centre of the town. For a long while, butter was the port's main commodity, with 3,000 barrels of Vale butter sent each year across the Channel to Bristol.[1] By 1536 Cardiff was accepted as the county town of Glamorganshire.

For a long while during the seventeenth and eighteenth centuries, the port of Cardiff was renowned as a centre of smuggling. Tobacco was the major illegal import, and so successful was the trade that, in 1752, customs officers were reporting the existence of nearly 100 tobacco shops in Cardiff and the surrounding area.[2]

The Herbert family were the principal landowners in and around Cardiff, but it was only when John Stuart, the 1st Marquess of Bute, married into the Herbert family that things really began to move forward. In 1778 he began renovating the castle, and by the end of the century the town could boast both a racecourse and a regular stagecoach link to London.

Despite this success, Cardiff still lagged some way behind Merthyr Tydfil and Swansea, the iron and copper capitals of the world. The 1801 census made it only the twenty-fifth-largest town in Wales but this was a situation the Butes were about to change.

Cardiff owed its growth and prosperity to the coal-mining industry of the hinterland – train after train after train, full of the 'black gold', made its way down the Rhondda and Rhymney Valleys to the sea.

The 2nd Marquess of Bute was born in 1793 and he it was who set about creating the modern town of Cardiff. The biggest problem facing the iron masters and coal owners of Wales was transporting their goods to market – the Marquess of Bute, by building an efficient deep-water dock at Cardiff, provided them with the means to do exactly that.

Bute Dock was opened in October 1839, linked to the ironworks and coal mines of South Wales by the Taff Vale Railway. With coal increasingly being demanded by shipowners and the Admiralty, Cardiff's prosperity and position as the port for the Rhondda Valleys was firmly assured.

One dock was never going to be enough, not once the coal began to roll like a giant black snowball towards the sea. The first part of East Bute Dock (the original dock now being called West Bute Dock) was opened in July 1855, followed by other phases over the next few years. It was inevitable that further development would soon be required and Roath Dock was opened in 1887.

Good 'Cardiff coal', as the commodity was known, was now being sent to every corner of the world. By the 1850s the port was exporting 750,000 tons each year. Ships and sailors of all nations thronged the docks and the dockland areas of the town. Places like Bute Street and Tiger Bay became famous the world over – rough, tough areas where disagreements and disputes were invariably settled with fists, clubs or even knives.

By 1881 Cardiff had overtaken Merthyr Tydfil and Swansea in size, with people flocking to the town to settle and make a living. Although, in the last quarter of the nineteenth century, Cardiff faced fierce opposition from Penarth and Barry, the presence of the Coal Exchange in Mount Stuart Square, close to the docks, ensured that Cardiff remained the centre for the administration of the coal trade. It was here, in 1907 on the floor of the Exchange, that Britain's first million-pound deal was struck.

WITH THE TEN TON SHUTE.

Working conditions
on the docks
– and in the mines
– were hard and
uncompromising,
a far cry from the
rather idealised
picture shown here.

Cardiff Docks at
night. Whatever
the time of day,
the work went on.
This shows the
Pier Head building
at the heart of the
enterprise.

By 1914 Cardiff was
a busy and bustling
city, full of traders
and merchants.
Here the statue of
John Bachelor, a
typical self-made
businessman from
the city, stands in
front of the new
municipal library.

In 1893 the University College, South Wales, was established in the town, and the elegant streets of 'uptown' Cardiff were being laid out. There was a real sense of civic pride and cultural awareness. Small wonder that, in 1905, Cardiff was awarded city status.

*

The Taff Vale Railway had carried its first trainload of coal to Cardiff in 1855, but just two years later a new railway company, the Rhymney Railway, also built a connection into the docks. This immediately brought the coal mines of Monmouthshire in to the orbit of Cardiff Docks and, as this new railway company was greatly favoured by the Bute family, its advent severely limited the Taff Vale's access to the essential coal tips at Cardiff.

The response of the directors of the Taff Vale Railway was to create another dock, a dock of their own, free from the control of the mighty Bute empire. They chose to do it at nearby Penarth, 1 mile away from the docks at Cardiff.

The 1801 census recorded the total population of Penarth as a mere seventy-one – fifty years on and the figure had increased only to 273. In the early 1850s the combined population of Penarth, Cogan and Llandough, the three parishes destined to become the town of Penarth, barely reached 400.[3]

With the decision having been made, the Penarth Harbour & Railway Company, under the leadership of Robert Clive, grandson of Clive of India, moved quickly. The Ely Tidal Harbour Bill and the Penarth Harbour, Dock and Railway Act of 1857 gave the company the right to lease, for 999 years, the area on both flanks of the River Ely, and thereby create a new dock.

Opening the Ely Tidal Harbour involved only a quick conversion of the lower reaches of the Ely River, and the building of a railway line to connect with the main Taff Vale line at Cardiff. It was soon open for trade. Creating the harbour on the northern side of Penarth Head, however, was a far more complex building process. Locally quarried stone was to be used for the jetties and ten coal staithes were planned, each of them capable of handling 150 tons per hour.

Work began in 1859 and the new dock was opened six years later. In the first year alone, Penarth Dock exported an amazing 273,996 tons of coal, a figure that increased to nearly a million in 1870 and to 2 million tons by 1882.[4]

The town of Penarth grew quickly around the new docks. Early residents were the workmen who poured into the area to help build the docks complex. Some came from England but most were from Ireland, and by 1861 the population of the town had increased fivefold to over 2,000.

Penarth, like the lower part of Bute Street in Cardiff, was a rough, dangerous and wild place in those early days. Housing shortages meant that what houses there were invariably held two or three families. Public houses and inns offered the only real entertainment, fights were common and, inevitably, there were outbreaks of infectious diseases, brought about by overcrowding or by sailors off the visiting ships.

Then came a new type of resident. Eager to escape the grime and filth of nearby Cardiff, businessmen – mostly the shipowners and coal merchants from the docks – began to build themselves spacious villas in the new town. These villas were set well away from the rowdier parts of Penarth, and were substantial dwellings where the businessmen and their families could enjoy the sea air and all the advantages that came with their wealth.

The docks at Penarth, sailing ships and schooners mixing easily with tramp steamers in this pre-war view.

STANWELL ROAD, PENARTH

The town of Penarth grew quickly and easily around the docks, and by 1914 the place was basking in its prosperity.

Penarth Pier, complete with paddle steamer at the landing stage on the seaward end, waiting to embark passengers on a day cruise to Weston or Ilfracombe.

Along roads like Marine Parade, their elegant houses stared out across the Bristol Channel in solemn isolation – and it was isolation, physical isolation, from the other residents of the town. The old adage of 'never the twain shall meet' could not be more accurately applied. They may have been few in number when compared to the total population of the town, but at one time, it was said, Penarth could boast more millionaires than any other community in Wales.

It was a curious combination: the rough and ready on one side of town, the elegant ladies and gentlemen on the other. It gave the community a strange, dislocated air. However, it was not just the people; Penarth itself had more than a little of the split personality about it.

The place was an industrial centre – there were docks and seamen enough to prove it. There was also a beach, though, and, after 1895, a pleasure pier. Paddle steamers called every day in the summer to take on passengers for Channel cruises, and visitors strolled along the pier's wooden decking, holding on to their straw boaters in the brisk sea air, promenading in the height of fashion. There were minstrel shows and band concerts, and the hotels, which soon sprouted like mushrooms in the town, were always full to bursting.

When war broke out in 1914, Penarth was like a self-satisfied adolescent, basking in the glow of success and pride. Compared to Cardiff, it was young and fresh and new. It seemed as if nothing could ever interfere with its continued rapid rise.

*

The town of Barry was situated just 7 miles to the west of Cardiff and, like Penarth, was a small village until it became caught up in the throes of industrialisation.

The area had first been inhabited by people of the Mesolithic and Neolithic Ages, and later by the Romans. Just off the coast was a small island, barely a mile in length, a place where Viking raiders had once wintered and which, by its very presence and position, was to become a hugely significant factor in the eighteenth-century creation of Barry Docks.

In the fourteenth century, Barry was a village and a port of some importance, but the place was ravaged by the Black Death in the second half of the century. The depredations of Owain Glyndŵr's rebellion in the early fifteenth century merely added to Barry's problems. The place took hundreds of years to recover, with Hearth Tax returns for 1673 indicating there were just thirteen houses in the village. As late as 1871 there were just twenty-one buildings, and the population hovered around the 100 mark.

Between Barry Island and the mainland lay Barry Sound, protected from the wild south-westerly winds by the island and by Friar's Point. It was a shallow stretch of water that had been the port in the Middle Ages, and it was this sheltered area of calm that attracted industrial developers.

Plans for a coal dock at Barry had been circulating for some time. As early as 1861, a letter to the *Cardiff and Merthyr Guardian* advocated building a railway line from Pencoed, near Bridgend, through Barry, to join up with other lines outside Penarth. A dock at Barry, it was said, could export coal and iron, and import foodstuffs such as hay and grain.[5]

The idea came to nothing, but years later David Davies, owner of Ocean Collieries, found himself and his business suffering from the Taff Vale Railway's limited capacity – just one double-line track down the valley after Pontypridd – and his mind turned to the old Barry scheme.

Davies would have liked to use Cardiff to export his coal. It was the closest port to his mines and was the logical choice, but that would have meant extending the dock facilities. The Marquess of Bute was quite happy with the work of Cardiff Docks as they were; they were more than sufficient for his needs and he saw no need to help someone who was a business rival. Davies, a self-made millionaire and not the man to back down from a confrontation, decided it was time for a new dock. Barry would come into its own.

The Barry Dock and Railway Bill was introduced during the 1883 session of parliament but, due to the influence of the Bute family, it was defeated. Undaunted, David Davies reintroduced the Bill the following year. This time, on 14 August 1884, it passed and was enshrined in law.

Construction of the docks, and the railway lines to service them, began as soon as the Bill was passed. No. 1 dock covered approximately 73 acres and was opened, along with the dock basin, in 1889. When it became clear that expansion was needed, the original dock was followed by a second deep-water dock in 1898.[6]

The growth of Barry Docks was rapid. By 1892 the old order had been swept away and Barry was already handling a third more coal than Cardiff. Barry Docks: it was the success story of the century. In 1913, they handled 11 million tons of coal, and Barry had become the largest coal-exporting port in the world. In that year alone, over 4,000 ships entered the port.

As with Penarth, houses had to be built to cater for the men building the docks and for those who stayed on to operate them. Always a working-class community, Barry nevertheless had many grand houses, most of them in the vicinity of Barry Island and Cold Nap. By the outbreak of the First World War the town consisted of over 200 streets and a population close on 40,000.

Barry Island – once the haunt of smugglers and pirates – had always been a popular spot for day trippers. As early as 1876 no fewer than 12,000 visitors flocked out to the island, making their way across the stepping stones that stretched from the mainland or embarking on one of the boats that plied a lucrative, if seasonal, trade to and from the island.

A by-product of the coming of the docks was the building of a causeway permanently linking Barry Island to the mainland. The railway station on the island opened in 1896, and from then on development was rapid. Cafés, tea rooms, shops and, in 1912, the Figure 8 ride at the new funfair all added to the attractions of the area.

Barry Island had always been popular, but in the wake of the new dock development it quickly became the main holiday destination in South Wales.

The amusements at Barry Island were rather 'downmarket' when compared to those at Penarth. There was no pleasure pier or elegant promenade, but for children and tired miners or steelworkers, down for the day from Merthyr, the funfair more than compensated. Then, of course, there was a sandy beach – something Penarth could certainly not boast.

In 1913 Barry, like the other coal ports of South Wales, had enjoyed its best ever year. Export of coal was at an all-time high and, as 1914 dawned, everyone in the town had reason to believe that nothing would change.

*

If, by 1914, Cardiff, Penarth and Barry were bustling, exciting places to live, the same could not be said for the rest of the Vale of Glamorgan. It was a quiet, rural backwater and it sometimes seemed as if things had not changed since the Normans first came to the area in the eleventh century.

The Vale was rich agricultural land, and in 1914 farming was still the main industry, with small, isolated holdings dotting the landscape. Most farmers held their land as tenants of the great landowners of the region, although, where it was available, access to common land was a much-prized right.

Communication was not easy, and the only form of transport was walking or maybe a lift on a farmer's hay cart. From villages like St Nicholas, although it lay on the main road into the city, Cardiff was still some 6 miles distant, down the steep gradient known as The Tumble. Going down might have been easy, coming back up was always a nightmare. Yet to the people who lived in these villages, Cardiff was just a short step away: 'Walking into the city was not uncommon … Sarah Ellis walked into Cardiff every Saturday to purchase her weekly groceries yet still arrived home in time to cook dinner for her family.'[7]

Until the sixteenth century, Aberthaw had been an important port, its ships regularly trading around the British coast and sometimes venturing as far as Spain and France. The chaos of the Civil War ended its significance and, despite the fact that there was some late smuggling activity, by 1914 this once bustling village had declined into a mud-locked, sleepy hamlet.

It was a similar story with Llantwit Major, a few miles to the west of Aberthaw. A monastery founded by St Iltyd in around AD 500 grew into a hugely important centre of learning in the post-Roman world. Scholars descended in droves on the college, where there were soon 400 teaching houses, and the small town of Llantwit Major grew up around them.

Despite being raided and burned by Vikings in AD 987, the monastery was rebuilt and, together with the town, survived until Henry VIII did what the Norse raiders had failed to do. With the Dissolution of the Monasteries in 1539, the centre of learning at Llantwit Major was wiped out with one stroke of the pen. The town remained but it was left without significance or purpose.[8]

Small communities such as St Bride's Major, Wick, St Athan and Llanblethian all had their churches, village pubs, village greens or ponds, but they were essentially tiny places where little happened and visitors seldom came.

The grand houses that had lorded it over the various communities for centuries, places like Cottrell, Wenvoe and Duffryn, were still there. Their owners, people like the Mackintosh,

Llantwit Major in the Vale. By 1914 the town had slid into a quiet and sedate old age despite its having been a renowned centre of learning in the ancient world.

Jenner and Cory families, still held sway, lords of all they surveyed. They hunted foxes in the season, shot pheasant and other game, and were deferred to by everyone – which was no more than they expected in what was, effectively, the last vestige of the old feudal system.

At Dunraven Castle on the coast at Southerndown, the Earl of Dunraven sat in solitary splendour. He was seventy-three years old when the First World War began, a man who was meant to have ridden with General Custer to fight the Sioux in 1869 – and would have done had not the invitation come a day too late. In 1914 he was still keen to 'do his bit.'[9]

The earl was aristocratic and did not tolerate fools gladly but he had the sort of personality that bred loyalty and a continuation of the rigid class system that existed in the Vale during these years. It did not stop him achieving a degree of popularity that is sometimes hard to understand.

By the early years of the twentieth century, the market town of Cowbridge was perhaps the most important part of the Vale's rural infrastructure but, no matter how important it was, the place was still small in size and population. The 1911 census returns, for example, give Cowbridge, at that time one of the larger communities in the Vale, a population of just over 1,000.[10]

Cowbridge, an ancient community, was one of the few medieval walled towns in Wales, and in the eighteenth century the writer Iolo Morgannwg, founder of the modern Eisteddfod, kept a bookshop in the town's single main street. Fine Georgian houses belonging to local families of note, people such as the Carnes and Edmondes, dominated the high street, and old coaching inns were still plying their trade.

This, then, was the Vale of Glamorgan when the guns of 1914 ended what must have seemed like an eternity of peace and quiet.

*

It would be wrong to say that, in the summer of 1914, no one expected war to break out. Conflict with Germany had been brewing for years as the Kaiser built up a fleet of Dreadnought

The market town of Cowbridge was perhaps the largest and most important Vale community outside of Penarth and Barry. Even so, its population had barely reached 1,000 in the years leading up to the First World War.

battleships to rival Britain's, while his attempts to extend the possessions of the German Empire were viewed with more than a degree of paranoia.

However, the 'naval race' was as much media-induced panic as reality, Germany always lagging behind in the building of new capital ships. As for Germany's Empire, so much of Africa and the Pacific had already been gobbled up by land-hungry European powers that there really was nowhere for the Germans to go – unless they acquired new territories by force of arms.

There had been rumblings and disquiet for weeks, ever since the news first broke about the assassination in Sarajevo on 28 June of the Archduke Franz Ferdinand, heir to the Austro-Hungarian throne. That was a European matter, though, not British, and nobody in Britain really expected the country to go to war over the death of one obscure foreign nobleman.

There was no denying that the situation in Europe was serious, with Germany, France, Austria-Hungary and Russia all engaged in fervent rounds of sabre rattling. The *South Wales Echo* for 25 July that year, under the trumpeting headline 'European War Threatened', sagely remarked that 'it is the general belief in diplomatic circles that never since 1870 has Europe been so near war as at the present moment'.[11]

That very same day, 25 July, the Austro-Hungarian government, as a punishment for what they saw as Serbian responsibility for the assassination, presented Serbia with an ultimatum, making such impossible demands that acceptance would have effectively ended the existence of Serbia as an independent nation. When these demands were not fully met, Austria-Hungary – supported by Germany – declared war on the smaller Balkan country.

A complicated series of alliances meant that if Germany's support of Austria-Hungary developed beyond mere words it would certainly bring France and Russia into conflict with Germany. The *South Wales Echo* again: 'Germany says that if a third power should intervene in a war between Austria and Servia [*sic*] her big battalions will be on the side of Austria.'[12]

At the end of July, Czar Nicholas 11th, seeing himself as the protector of all Slav people, gave the order for Russia to mobilise. Her huge standing army was quickly gathered together and

Above left: The assassination of Archduke Franz Ferdinand in June 1914 was the spark that fanned the flames of war. For many years this picture was thought to catch the arrest of Gavrilo Princip, the assassin, although doubt has recently been cast on that statement. It does, however, certainly show the capture of one of the conspirators.

Above right: One of the many recruiting posters that deliberately used the 'Remember Belgium' maxim to attract would-be soldiers.

sent to face the expected German assault along the border. France had already warned that, should Russia and Germany come to blows, her treaty obligations would force her to join a war against Germany. Despite this, on 1 August Germany declared war on Russia, and almost before people knew it the whole of Europe was at war.

Germany, now faced with the prospect of a war on two fronts, demanded free passage of her troops through Belgium so that she could attack France before the big French battalions were ready. Belgium refused but the German juggernaut rolled anyway, pummelling the Belgian frontier forts and driving deeply into enemy territory.

British politicians and newspapers, until now standing on the sidelines, invoked an old and largely forgotten treaty guaranteeing Belgian neutrality, to whip up war fever in the country. An ultimatum was issued, the Germans did not respond, and at midnight on 4 August 1914 Britain declared war on Germany.

Over the next few months, thousands of men went to their deaths believing that they had taken up arms in order to protect helpless little Belgium. The truth was that, once the other great powers went for each other's throats, Britain simply could not afford to stay out of the conflict. Whichever side won, once the war was over the balance of power in Europe would be changed for ever.

A victorious France, traditionally Britain's enemy – even though now, thanks to the Entente Cordiale, officially an ally – did not bear too much consideration. However, the thought of an all-powerful Germany – dominant in central Europe and with a newly acquired, much enlarged empire – sent shivers down the spines of every government minister. Hence the ultimatum and the charade of saving 'gallant little Belgium'.

2

And so to War

There might not yet have been war fever as such in the city, but by the middle of July 1914 the people of Cardiff and the Vale had been aware for a few weeks that something was amiss on the Continent. Whether or not Britain became involved was another matter, yet to be decided.

Then, on 15 July 1914, the *South Wales Echo* issued what was really a warning when it reported on the recalling of Britain's Naval Reservists, men who had served their allotted time with the fleet and were now simply waiting in reserve. Being a Reservist was, most of these men thought, just a paper exercise; nobody would ever call them back to the colours. They were wrong:

> Nearly 14,000 men of the Royal Fleet Reserves will today report themselves at the Naval Depots of Portsmouth, Chatham and Devonport. Every available officer and man will be withdrawn from the educational establishments – the gunnery, torpedo, navigation and signalling schools, and the War College – and almost the whole of our naval forces in home waters will be fully manned and placed – nominally at all events – on a war footing.[1]

Recalling the Reservists, for both Army and Navy, was a precautionary step as far as the government was concerned. Britain was the only European power not to have a system of conscription and these time-served men were actually a crucial part of Britain's defence network. They might not serve on the front line or in the newest ships of the Grand Fleet but, by their presence, they would release other men to do exactly that. At least, that was the theory.

On 3 August, with Britain's ultimatum for Germany to leave Belgium already issued and war now becoming more certain with every passing hour, Cardiff saw its first large gathering of Naval Reservists. For this first time at least, the departure of men to a possible war situation resulted in moments of wild abandon:

> Cardiff GWR Station was the scene of great enthusiasm as the various contingents from neighbouring towns arrived to entrain for Devonport, Plymouth and other naval depots. About sixty men were called up from Cardiff and their arrival with their friends and relatives at the station approach soon caused a very large crowd to gather … The enthusiastic crowd grew to such proportions that the station gates had to be closed and a posse of police was introduced to the platform to regulate the crowd.[2]

"With mad appeal to the Lord
A Tyrant draws his sword."

CARDIFF, PIER HEAD.

Above left: Anti-German propaganda reached new heights during the first few months of the war. As this cartoon postcard shows, the Kaiser was widely regarded as the arch villain of the piece.

Above right: Once war was declared in August 1914, Cardiff Docks immediately went into overdrive, sending coal to Admiralty bases all over the world.

At 11.30 that night, just before the midnight deadline, the train finally pulled out. About 300 men were packed into the carriages and they left with repeated cheers ringing in their ears. It was not all enthusiasm, however: 'In the crowd there were many seriously visaged people and many women who were moved to tears at the call for their husbands and sons.'[3]

Half an hour later Britain was at war. Over the next few days the scene was repeated several times as trains full of Reservists returning to their units, ships or depots left Cardiff. The wives and mothers might weep but in most of Cardiff, as in the rest of Britain, the declaration of war was met mainly with great approval.

Suddenly Cardiff streets were full of soldiers and sailors, most of whom seemed to have a girl on each arm. Being a port, merchant seamen as well as men from the Royal Navy were suddenly feted and treated to drinks in the city pubs. A month earlier, such men were barely noticed, maybe even shunned. Now they were the new heroes of the Empire:

> I never saw much of Cardiff the one time my father took me on a trip to Barry. We went into Cardiff on the train, then out again so all I really saw was the station.
>
> But I do remember, as we pulled in, we were high up. You know, the line was, what do you call it, elevated. I looked down – and it was just before the river, before the old Cardiff

Arms Park. There were soldiers walking, lounging on the pavements with girls hanging onto them. They looked ever so happy, ever so important. The girls all wore big fancy bonnets, if I remember rightly.

There were lots of big men there as well, strong men with reefer jackets over their shoulders. 'Sailors,' father said, 'men from the docks. Bute Street's only over there.' He pointed and I felt a flutter in my stomach. Well it was a rough old area, Bute Street. It was famous. Part of me wanted to go and see it, part of me was just too afraid.

As it happened I had no chance. Father was on business, he didn't have time for things like sight seeing. So it was off to Barry, Cardiff had to wait. It must have been twenty years before I went back.[4]

Despite the enthusiasm for the war, in these early days a mild form of panic fell across the city – after all, who knew where the Germans might suddenly strike!

Four German ships, in port at Cardiff on the day war was declared, were seized – arrested was the term used. Their cargoes were impounded, the crews imprisoned and the vessels searched for hidden arms. To the consternation of the authorities, very few guns were actually discovered on the ships, but in the eyes of the police and Army it was better safe than sorry.

It has been estimated that in the summer of 1914 no fewer than 35,000 Germans were living in Britain – when many of them went back to Germany to fight for their homeland, they left wives and sweethearts behind. If they weren't quick enough, however, they faced the same fate as the sailors. The Aliens Registration Act was rushed through Parliament the day after war broke out, and by the autumn nearly 14,000 Germans and Austrians were languishing in British internment camps.

Armed guards were stationed at Cardiff Docks and at other places of importance as soon as war was declared. All ships were stopped and searched before entering, a special fleet of pilot boats and tugs being assembled for the task. On the night of 6 August, there was an incident that was guaranteed to have all innocent citizens quaking in their shoes: 'During last night a man was challenged at Llanishen Reservoir by one of the armed men on guard. He refused to answer but took to his heels. He was shot at but got away.'[5]

The man was probably no more than a simple poacher but the fact that he was shot at was positive proof of the seriousness of the situation – it is not hard to imagine the fright of the poor poacher suddenly facing gunshots rather than a gamekeeper's cudgel. The fear of German spies and saboteurs remained powerful for many months to come.

As the German advance drove deeper into Belgium, South Wales saw its first Belgian refugees, men and women fleeing from the carnage of the battlefield. By early October, Cardiff was housing 165 of them – Barry had 100, Penarth 75. Soon it was estimated that the total number of refugees in Wales was over 1,000.

To begin with there was no reason to suppose that the war would be fought, as all wars of the past had been fought, by anything other than Regular soldiers and Reservists. There was just one difference. The Liberal government had, in 1906, reformed the Army, when the Secretary of State for War, the Rt Hon. R. B. Haldane, replaced the old yeomanry units, which had for years been the bulwark of home defence, with a new territorial force. It was a volunteer organisation attached to each county regiment and was intended for service at home. Members were 'part-time soldiers' who trained at the weekends or in the evenings and, each summer, took part in a two-week camp.[6]

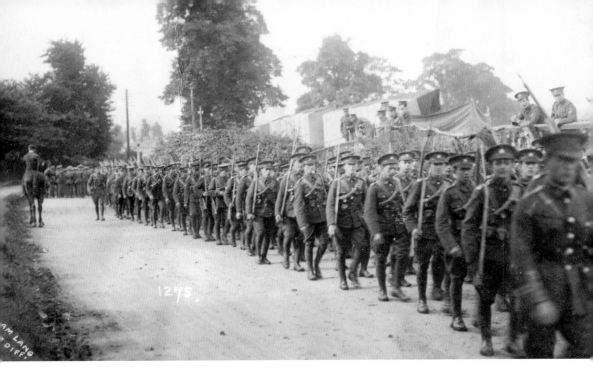

Soldiers marching through Cardiff in the first few months of the war. Wherever they went, soldiers like these were greeted with flag-waving crowds and loud cheers.

The Terriers, as they were called, were hugely popular. In the days before wireless and television, membership of this unique organisation brought men kudos and, at the very basic level, gave them something to do in their leisure hours.

The British Army, in relation to those of other nations, was tiny – 250,000 men compared with 800,000 in Germany and a million plus in Russia. However, in August 1914 many of these soldiers were serving in far-flung corners of the Empire; it would take months to get them back. Even with Reservists and Territorials called to the colours, it was obvious that, if Britain was going to honour her treaty obligations, there was an urgent need for volunteers.[7]

They came in their thousands. The almost universal desire to give the Kaiser 'the bloody nose he so richly deserved' meant that the recruiting stations were inundated. It was a time of white feathers for men not in uniform, a time of free drinks in the pubs for all soldiers and sailors. Cardiff and the surrounding area was no different from the rest of Britain: 'The response to the call for volunteers for the Welsh Horse has exceeded expectations. Up to this morning almost 1500 had enrolled but only 1200 are needed.'[8]

The press gleefully joined in the fun, urging young men to join up, to enjoy a new experience and see something of the world. On the very day that war was declared, the editorial columns of the *Western Mail*, the national newspaper of Wales, were declaring, 'Let it not be recorded to our eternal shame that young men were playing cricket and football while the nation's call for soldiers continued unfulfilled.'[9]

The *Penarth Times* was even more unequivocal. That August the paper ran an article under the headline 'Clear Out the Cowards'. Drawing on the theme that, if the Germans could behave so abominably to poor, defenceless little Belgium, Britain had no chance if they ever landed

Lord Kitchener, Secretary of State for War, delivers his famous recruiting slogan.

here, the editor left readers in no doubt where the paper stood on the subject: 'Our young men go about in their tennis rig-outs or parade on the Esplanade, smirking at girls. Is it fair that they should go about so callously whilst those who took up arms, with our promised support, lie cold and stiff … give the laggards their marching orders.'[10]

*

Penarth Docks, like those at Cardiff, were given extra protection, even before war broke out. Starting on 3 August, all ships wishing to enter the port were stopped outside the dock gates, their captains questioned and, if it was felt necessary, the vessels searched. Police guarding the dock installations were quickly armed and reinforced, and even the local branch of the National Union of Women's Suffrage announced that, for the time being at least, it had suspended its political actions and placed its members at the service of the local authorities.[11]

In Penarth itself there was, as in Cardiff, considerable enthusiasm for the war, and by the end of August the town had given over 400 of its men to the Army and Royal Navy. Yet the war was not uniformly popular in the town:

> On Sunday evening last, at Stanwell Road Baptist Chapel, the pastor, the Rev Gwilym O Griffiths, made a special reference to the war and in no uncertain manner protested against England being implicated in the present hostilities between Russia, France and Germany. A resolution was passed deploring the European crisis.[12]

The Revd Griffiths must have had a dramatic change of heart, as he later served as a padre in France, speaking eloquently about the qualities of the British soldiers he encountered and the righteousness of what they were doing.

Perhaps more importantly for the households of the town, the price of flour had increased, loaves of bread rising in price by one penny, and there was clear evidence of panic buying:

> The war is having a serious effect upon local trade. In some trades the assistants are working early and late to cope with the orders received. This applies especially to grocers, who have had their stocks reduced by persons with money laying in large stocks of provisions. Already many articles have increased enormously in price, especially flour, bacon, tea, sugar, rice and tinned goods, upon which there has been a remarkable run.[13]

There had been large numbers of visitors to Penarth during the early summer, but once war was declared the town seemed to empty overnight as people decamped back home. It did not augur well for the town's tourist trade over the coming months. People working on the railways and in the Post Office in the town had had all their leave cancelled for the foreseeable future.

Two brothers from the town, Wilfred and Ernest Guy, had been in Switzerland when war broke out. Trying to get back to Britain they found that all passenger services had been suspended because of hostilities. Undaunted, the brothers rode on the footboards of goods trains across the Swiss border, and managed to make it as far as Paris before they were 'put off'. They somehow managed to catch a train to Amiens, and eventually found a boat to take them to Folkestone. They spent three nights sleeping in the corridors of the trains but eventually reached home – in time to enlist!

Meanwhile, back in Penarth, spy scares were the talk of the town. On 27 August a German sailor off one of the ships in the dock, a man who had somehow escaped arrest by the authorities, was apprehended by one of the Army Reservists who was now stationed at the docks. The man was taken to the police station where he was detained overnight before being sent away for internment.

Then came something rather more serious:

> The usual peaceful calm of the residents near St Augustine's Church was disturbed on Wednesday morning by the sudden firing of shots, and some alarm was at first felt. It appears that a sentry on duty near the church was fired on by someone who shielded himself behind the bushes in the enclosure facing St Augustine's Road. The sentry quickly responded with a couple of shots in the direction where the shot had been fired but the culprit managed to make good his escape.[14]

The area was immediately searched but nothing – and no one – was ever found. An imaginative sentry, spooked by the wind and early morning shadows, one of the soldier's mates playing a game, or a real-life enemy agent? The riddle has never been solved.

The spy scares continued. In the late summer, an unknown man was seen walking along Windsor Road in the town, asking questions about the deployment of troops. He was followed by Mr A. I. Beer until, realising he was being shadowed, the man took to his heels. Mr Beer gave chase for over 2 miles until the man was eventually lost in the warren of streets in the Riverside area of Cardiff.[15]

In December another man was seen prowling close to the power station in the docks. Challenged, he pulled out a gun, fired twice and ran off. Such stories probably say more about the over-imaginative minds of sentries and the public than they do about the realities of spies or saboteurs, but they offer an intriguing insight into the emotional state of Penarth residents at this time.

Perhaps a more pertinent – and altogether sadder – insight into the state of the town, indeed the state of the nation, was captured in a letter written by a Mr Jules Guldentops to the *Penarth Times* on 27 August:

Dear Sir – I have been taken for a German many times and I am very sorry to see the public is under a mis-apprehension as to my nationality. I was born in Mons, Belgium. I came to Cardiff 27 years ago. My wife is a native of Wales. After being so many years in Great Britain, with the British public, I call myself a British patriot. Yours truly, Jules Guldentops, 7 Lord Street, Penarth.[16]

The real tragedy of Mr Guldentops is not that he suffered from abuse and obvious harassment, but the fact that he felt he had to write the letter in the first place. It clearly was an intolerant and difficult time if you had a German-sounding name.

The need to attract special constables to patrol the streets and swell the number of regular policemen was first brought to the notice of the populace soon after war broke out, with the news that no fewer than 30,000 citizens were to be enrolled as constables in the Metropolitan Police area. Then, on 25 August 1914, the *Penarth Advertiser* reported that 'on Saturday evening upwards of fifty residents were sworn in as Special Constables at the police court in Penarth'.[17]

It was not all hardship. A company of Garrison Artillery had fitted up searchlights on the end of Penarth Pier as early as 2 August. Each night the lights, deliberately operated from water level to give a better beam, swept the waters off Penarth, searching for any U-boats or surface raiders that might come near. They never did, but for the people of Penarth the light show was great entertainment. When war broke out, concerts in the Bijou Pavilion at the seaward end of the pier had been cancelled so it was good to have at least some form of entertainment: 'The searchlights nightly attract a large concourse of people on the promenade and in the park, and in part compensate for the loss of the strains of music so much enjoyed on Thursday evenings.'[18]

As the year drew to a close, the war of movement in France and Belgium ground to a halt. Soldiers 'dug in', hewing long, water-sodden trenches from the Flanders clay. It was a back-breaking, unpleasant task, and many Penarth men wrote home telling relatives and friends about their experiences.

Some of those letters found their way into the *Penarth Times*, either sent directly to the paper or passed on by the original recipients. There was little or no attempt at censorship in this early part of the war and, by reading the letters, a realistic and graphic account of the lives of soldiers can be pieced together:

The trench digging … is costing us a few men. We have had one wounded in both legs today, and last week we had two wounded. This is a short life but a grey one, I am thinking. Still we must hope for the best.[19]

Life in the trenches – not quite what the men who enlisted in August and September 1914 had in mind!

I have not known what it is to have a dry foot for eight days for it has been raining day and night. The trenches get flooded and in places we have to be over our knees in water and mud. Our sleeping places get very wet.[20]

It is a horrible war. People would not believe half the things that happen unless they were to see for themselves.[21]

I have had my baptism of fire and am now away behind the lines having a rest. We were under fire for two and a half days. It's a wonder to me that anything could live under such a rain of bullets like that … I was lying on the ground, flat on top of the hill, for about two hours, digging myself in as best I could with bullets flying over me. I can tell you, I never felt more uncomfortable in my life.[22]

This was certainly not the war men had enlisted for. Moreover, it was not the war their relatives and other civilians back home in Penarth expected to hear about.

*

Monday 3 August 1914 was a beautiful day in South Wales, and at Barry Island, on this last day of peace for over four years, it seemed that people did not have a care in the world. It was August Bank Holiday and, as was later estimated, close on 50,000 day trippers flocked to the island to enjoy the sunshine and the sand. There was a brass band competition on Nells Point, and people sat easily on deckchairs or just lay on the grass, gazing at the cloudless sky.

It was a day of leisure – for some but not for all. With war looming, the Lords of the Admiralty needed their coal stocks high, and requested that the trimmers and dockers at Barry work throughout the bank holiday. Between 1 and 4 August these men loaded no fewer than 200,000 tons of coal into Admiralty colliers.[23] Of course, they were well rewarded for their efforts.

Within a few short hours of dusk on 3 August, as the government deadline to Germany approached, the holidaymakers left Barry, and things had changed beyond all recognition. Now it was the working up of the 6-inch guns at Barry Fort on Nells Point, rather than the performance of the bands, that caught people's attention. Just like Penarth, huge searchlights were installed to sweep the sea lanes.

On 4 August a German steamer, the *Ulla Boog*, a regular caller at Barry with wood for pit props, came into port. She had no radio, and her captain and crew had no idea that war had been declared. She was immediately detained as a war prize. Sold by auction and renamed the *Mary Baird*, she was an unlucky ship, being sunk after striking a mine off the coast of Cornwall in 1917.[24]

Barry's Naval Reservists had already marched away before war began, but the three Territorial units based in the town – the Glamorgan Fortress Engineers, a company of the Royal Garrison Artillery and the Welsh Royal Cyclists – were also now mobilised. These were the men who would be stationed along the Welsh coast of the Bristol Channel for what were termed the Severn Defences.

On 10 August fifty German seamen from ships in the docks, men who had been marooned when war was declared, appeared before the local magistrates. Although they had done nothing wrong, they were detained for the duration. By September it was estimated that around 200 German sailors had been interned in Cardiff, Penarth and Barry.

It was a time of some hysteria in Barry. That August, three days after war began, a young schoolteacher, Edward Thomas Davies, was apprehended while sketching in the vicinity of Barry Fort. He was charged with making sketches in a prohibited area, sketches that could be of use to the enemy – although quite what use German Zeppelin pilots would have made of them is a matter of conjecture.

It later transpired that Davies was making his sketches as part of an exercise for a summer art school at Barry College. Nevertheless his drawings were destroyed, he was issued with a severe reprimand and he was lucky to escape a custodial sentence.[25]

By 17 August 1914 the vast majority of the British Expeditionary Force, close on 90,000 troops, had managed to cross to France, and several Barry men, mostly Reservists, were with them. The first Barry man to die in the war was Private J. W. Turner of the Welsh Regiment, but as he had not yet gone to France he was at least able to spend his final days at home.

The Battle of Mons on 23 August was the first real British engagement of the war. Two British divisions were attacked by larger German forces when accurate and rapid fire from the British infantry convinced the Germans they were facing a machine-gun company. The German advance stuttered but when the French battalions on the British flank began to withdraw, leaving the BEF in danger of being cut off, Sir John French, their commander, had no alternative but to fall back.[26]

It was a hard fighting retreat in which several Barry men were involved. Signaller Albert Rees Hunt, later to die of wounds, told the *Barry Dock News*, 'The Battle of Mons was terribly

The British Expeditionary Force left for France within two weeks of war breaking out, all the men happy to take part in giving the Kaiser 'a bloody nose'. This composite set of photographs shows units of the BEF coming ashore at Boulogne.

*Sketches
of Tommy's life*
In Training. — Nº 1

" That seems to mean me all right "

The need to supplement the Regular Army was soon apparent, and all manner of devices were used to get men to enlist – even the humble postcard. This drawing by Fergus MacKain clearly tells everyone what they should do.

The battle and subsequent retreat from Mons was the first time British and German troops came face to face in the war. Several Barry men, Reservists and Territorials, were involved in the confrontation.

fierce and the British soldiers marched 200 miles in twelve days, snatching whatever rest wherever we could. It was very little though.'[27]

The first Barry man to die in action was a sailor, Warrant Officer William Cowling, who was serving on the cruiser *Hawke* when she was torpedoed by a U-boat in the North Sea on 15 October 1914. Only sixty sailors were rescued from the *Hawke*, and Cowling was not among them.[28]

When news of the British Naval defeat at the Battle of Coronel reached Barry, it was an anxious time for the relatives of men serving on the British cruisers: 'Several men from Barry were on board the cruiser "Monmouth," and up to this morning their relatives had received no official information from the Admiralty as to their fate.'[29]

Sadly, the old and outdated *Monmouth*, like her companion the *Good Hope*, was lost with all hands in the icy waters of the southern Atlantic. Among the Barry men who were killed in the disaster were engine room artificers Thomas Watkins and Robertson Horsham, and stokers John Keniry and George Thomas Russell.

The German advance through Belgium and northern France seemed, at first, to be unstoppable. Even after they were halted at the Battle of the Marne and then pushed back to a line along the River Aisne, the coal-mining areas of France and Belgium remained in their hands. The supply of Welsh coal was clearly going to be crucial, and Barry, the largest coal-exporting port in the world, now assumed major significance.

The armoured cruiser *Monmouth* sunk at the Battle of Coronel in 1914. It was Britain's first naval defeat in over a hundred years. At least four Barry men went down with the *Monmouth* when she was sunk with all hands.

At the outbreak of war, control of all railways and docks was taken over by the government – it meant a virtual guarantee of work in Barry Docks for the duration of the war. It was not just the export of coal that occupied the dockers at Barry, there were many imports as well: 'Huge stores were set up containing timber for the pits and hay for use abroad; imported grain was stored in two large sheds. Thousands of Naval and military transports were loaded with raw materials, equipment and munitions.'[30]

There was a great influx of soldiers into the town, which, right to the end of hostilities when regiments of American doughboys finally arrived, offered a safe port of embarkation for troops. To begin with, the incoming troops were billeted in schools and church halls, but in October 1914 work began on a large hutted camp at Buttrills on the edge of the town. By November it was completed, and the 12th Battalion of the Welsh Regiment became the first occupants.

Within the town itself, recruiting was initially quite slow but, by the end of 1914, over 1,400 Barry men had enlisted – including nineteen members of the Barry Male Voice Choir.[31] In the aftermath of the war, at the Peace Day Celebrations in 1919, Howell Williams, Chair of the Council, estimated that 15,000 Barry men had served with the colours – not all volunteers, of course, many of those men being conscripted after 1916 – and, of these, he estimated some 700 had died.[32]

Perhaps most significantly of all, Barry – as a dock and port town – was home to many merchant sailors. Of these, at least 261 died during the war, their names now recorded on the Barry Merchant Navy Memorial outside the town's civic centre. The greatest loss of life came in 1917, when 136 Barry merchant seamen died, 93 following in 1918.[33] Seafaring had always been a dangerous profession, but such losses were hard to bear.

*

In the rural parts of the Vale of Glamorgan, recruiting was almost as brisk as it was in the three large towns. In many cases it was led by the sons of the great houses or, as in the case of someone like Miles Bruce Dalzell, by the sons of the clergy. Dalzell, from the Old Rectory in St Nicholas, served as a lieutenant with the Highland Light Infantry and, a year later, was killed in the conflict.[34]

Cowbridge, as one of the larger communities, had more than its fair share of early recruits, particularly once Lord Kitchener's famous recruiting poster began to work its magic. In September 1914 over twenty volunteers gathered together at Cowbridge station, all dressed in their best, ready to head off for the training depots. They did not know it at the time but several of them were leaving the town for ever.

Private Alexander Pates, a Reservist recalled to the colours with the 2nd Welsh Regiment, was the town's first casualty. He died of wounds received during fighting in what was soon to be labelled 'the Salient' at Ypres on 26 October 1914. Arthur Wynne Jones and Frank Dunn, from Cowbridge and Llanblethian respectively, died on 10 August 1915, two days after the 5th Welsh stormed the beaches at Suvla Bay during the Gallipoli Campaign.[35]

Some Vale men were luckier. They survived, even if it was as prisoners of war, as Harry Griffith Jenkins from St Athan later recalled:

antwit Road St Athan 1597 M

Many men from the tiny village of St Athan enlisted to fight or, as Reservists, were called back to the colours in August 1914.

My uncle, Glover Griffiths, my mother's brother, was in the Royal Artillery and went across to France. He was captured, held prisoner till the end of the war. When he came back we'd ask him, us kids, how it had all gone. 'Well,' he'd say, 'we fired our gun till it was red hot. Then the officer told us to rip up everything we had, we were prisoners.'

The other St Athan man I can remember was Jack Duckett. He was taken prisoner right at the beginning of the war. When he came home we gave him a procession through the village.

I must have been seven at the time and I can remember making dip sticks, dipping sticks into tar, then setting them alight. We made a procession for Jack, holding our dip sticks out in front of us, the flames billowing in the night sky. Jack loved telling us tales. 'I remember treading on my own hair,' he used to say. 'It was that long.'[36]

Nobody in the Vale knew what to expect in the war. They just knew that they had to be a part of it. 'Home by Christmas' was the adage. The only trouble was that nobody said which Christmas they were thinking about.

3

The Cardiff Pals

On 6 August 1914, Lord Kitchener, the hero of the Sudan and avenger of Gordon of Khartoum, was appointed Secretary of State for War. If the government thought they were getting a 'yes man', they were much mistaken. Kitchener, in total contrast to everyone else in a position of power, knew that this war against Germany would be a long and protracted conflict.

He proposed raising a huge volunteer army to support the Regulars, and suggested that as many as 100,000 men might be needed. It was a target that was easily reached, and overtaken many times. In what was a unique and, as far as numbers were concerned, highly successful recruiting drive, the concept of Pals Battalions was born.

The Pals were units of volunteers who were promised that, if they enlisted, they could serve alongside their friends and work colleagues rather than being shipped off to fill gaps in Regular Army battalions. The authorities, of course, conveniently forgot that, if men could enlist and serve together, they could also die together.

The original name did not come from Kitchener, although he quickly seized on the term. It was first coined by the Earl of Derby, who raised a battalion of 1,500 men in Liverpool. He said, 'This should be a battalion of pals, a battalion in which friends from the same office will fight shoulder to shoulder for the honour of Britain and the credit of Liverpool.'[1]

It was a sentiment with which many young men agreed. Cardiff, along with fifty other cities and towns across Britain, immediately began to raise a Pals battalion. They were the 11th Battalion, Welsh Regiment, the Cardiff Commercials, better known as 'The Pals'. Commanded by Colonel F. Russel Parkinson, the volunteer soldiers were shopworkers and solicitors, schoolteachers, coal miners and dockers – as one national newspaper used to say, all human life was there.

The main recruiting centre for the unit was Gladstone Road School and, to begin with, the volunteers lived at home, reporting to Maindy Barracks on a daily basis. They had no rifles and no uniforms, a badge on their lapels being the only sign of corporate identity. Many businesses, only too happy to support the Pals, awarded family allowances to the wives of men who enlisted, some firms even putting their senior workers on half pay for the duration of the war.[2] It was a useful addendum to the basic Army pay.

On 14 September 1914 the Pals left Cardiff, 750 men marching in straw boaters and bowler hats through the city streets to the railway station. Their destination was Lewes and then to a tented camp at Seaford. Like other soldiers of the time, many of the Pals wrote letters home or to the papers, describing their experiences of training for war: 'So far we have had glorious

Don't be Alarmed, the Cardiff Pals are on guard

The Cardiff Pals, one of many similar battalions raised in towns and cities across Britain, brought together a wide assortment of men, all eager to 'do their bit' – from dockers and steelworkers to farmers and city clerks.

weather. Every morning before 7-o-clock, the Battalion are off to drill at the double, and for an hour the platoons are quick marching, hopping and doubling round their rough training ground to the sharp command of the instructors.'[3]

Slowly and gradually, the Pals were learning the ropes about soldiering. Like all similar battalions, the Cardiff Pals was a mix of men who might otherwise never speak to each other in civilian life, as one man described when writing to the *South Wales Echo*:

> The Battalion has been provided this week with some old Lee-Enfield rifles. During drills the men left in camp may be seen in the lines, helping each other with the rifles and practicing aiming. You see the 'knuts' of the city and Docks struggling with tufts of grass and earth to remove grease from the dinner 'dickie,' and sticking knives and forks into the ground to get the desirable freshness to those articles ready for another meal.[4]

'Knuts', a term that has now disappeared, meant young men who fancied themselves as fashionable dandies.

The weather soon turned wet and the camp at Seaford was transformed into a morass of mud. Spirits, however, remained high, even though some letters seemed designed more for public morale than descriptions of reality:

> Twelve in a tent is hardly a crowd and when those twelve are all out to help each other you can imagine how happy we are. Some of the tents have been given names. There is 'The Suicide Club' and this tent is decorated with skeletons and deathly looking bones. Other names are as follows – 'Gamblers Den,' 'The Vicarage,' (next door to each other), 'Cook House View' … and several more. We named our little den 'The Twelve Apostles.'[5]

The trenches, shown here after a battle. The cost, in terms of lives and equipment, was astronomical.

In May 1915 the Cardiff Pals, part of the 22nd Division, moved to Aldershot prior to service overseas. On 4 September they sailed from Southampton to Le Havre, the whole battalion standing on deck, singing a Welsh hymn: 'Clanging, banging and riveting and all other noises of a port at war were suddenly silent. It was a deeply moving experience and survivors of the 11th Welsh, to a man, recall it without prompting. As some said "It was Wales going to war."'[6]

In late September they took up position in the front line on the Somme and, inevitably, began to suffer casualties. Their service in France, however, was short-lived, as that October they received orders to take ship to Salonika in Macedonia. The battalion sailed from Marseilles on 30 October, arriving nine days later at a town of shimmering minarets and gaily painted houses. To the Cardiff Pals, at first sight, it looked like an earthly paradise. How wrong they were.

The campaign in Macedonia can be justifiably called 'the forgotten campaign' of the First World War. It had little strategic importance, apart from tying down German and Bulgarian troops who could have been usefully employed elsewhere. To the Cardiff Pals, however, the place was a hellhole. In a country where the environment was as much an enemy as the Germans who faced them – always staring down from huge mountain heights onto the British below – this was a war of attrition.

For the next three years the Cardiff Pals were involved in the most costly 'sideshow' of what was then the most costly war in history: 'A sideshow, yes, that was it! But what a place to stage it, where winter brought 20 degrees of frost and summer tipped the thermometer well over 100 degrees. Where a man could die from frostbite – or malaria.'[7]

In those three years the Cardiff Pals took casualties, endured boredom on a monumental scale and tried their best to survive. Private 'Stokey' Lewis from Milford Haven – presumably he had been working in Cardiff when the war broke out – won the Victoria Cross for rescuing an officer wounded in a trench raid, and there were dozens of other examples of bravery and heroism.

It all culminated on 18 September 1918 – a few months before the war ended – in a suicidal, frontal assault on the Grande Couronne in the Dorian sector of the front. The enemy knew they were coming, they were dug in and virtually unassailable. Yet the attack had to be made

After a brief period on the Western Front, the Cardiff Pals were sent to take part in the campaign in Salonika, a costly and now largely forgotten episode in the history of the war.

and, inevitably, the result was slaughter: 'The cream of Cardiff's young men, a finely tempered fighting battalion, at 5 a.m. lay dead, dying or wounded three hours later when the sun rose, blood red, over the Grande Couronne.'[8]

The real tragedy of the battle was that four days later, when reconnaissance patrols went out, they found that the Bulgarian defenders of the Grande Couronne had abandoned their posts and retreated.

Nearly 150 Cardiff Pals died in the campaign in Macedonia, part of a forgotten army that never received one portion of the recognition it deserved. Only the men themselves and their families back home in Cardiff and the surrounding districts knew the real cost of what they had achieved.

*

As well as the Cardiff Pals (Commercials), Cardiff also raised a second 'Pals' battalion, this one being the 16th Welsh (Cardiff City) Battalion.

On 19 September 1914, six weeks after the war began, David Lloyd George gave a speech at the Queen's Hall in London, calling for the formation of a separate Welsh army. Three weeks later the War Office agreed that the National Executive Committee could take responsibility for the recruiting and organisation of a Welsh Army Corps.

Several Battalions were already in the process of being formed under what were known as 'local initiatives', but permission was refused to incorporate already formed units – such as the 11th Welsh, Cardiff Pals, Commercial – into this new Welsh Army Corps.[9]

On 2 November 1914 the National Executive Committee called on the Lord Mayor of Cardiff to raise a completely new battalion. The Mayor, Alderman J. T. Richards, promptly agreed, and on 23 November recruiting began. Captain Frank Gaskell, recuperating at home from wounds, was promoted to colonel and given command of the battalion.

Unfortunately, the initial enthusiasm for the war – or, at least, the initial enthusiasm to enlist for the war – had waned somewhat. Those in control quickly found that, with many of the more adventurous men already serving in the 11th Battalion – the original Cardiff Pals – it was no longer easy to recruit a thousand men.

Public meetings were held, and there were also appeals at soccer matches and in music halls. Concerts of military band music proved to be one of the more successful schemes for recruitment. Advertisements were also taken out, and articles in papers such as *The Barry Herald* in December 1914 were not above the use of veiled (or not so veiled) threats to achieve the desired effect: 'We don't want conscripts in Barry; therefore come forward now as volunteers, and make conscription unnecessary.'[10]

Recruitment in Cardiff, and in the other communities across the Vale of Glamorgan, was slow and steady, rather than spectacular. However, as 1914 eased into the new year of 1915, the target number was tantalisingly close: 'The recruiting barometer of the Cardiff City Battalion continues to rise at a steady rate. By Monday evening the strength of the battalion had reached about 750 and Colonel Gaskell and his co-workers feel hopeful of good returns during the next few days.'[11]

The Cardiff City Battalion was never intended to be an exclusively 'Cardiff' unit, as men came from all over Wales. The whole range of society was represented. There were strong connections with Cardiff Rugby Club, with a number of internationals joining up. These included John L. Williams, Bert Weifield and Clem Lewis. The club's former vice captain, Fred Smith, became second-in-command of the battalion. Glamorgan police were also well represented, with men such as Dick Thomas and James Angus duly taking their places in the ranks.

Finally, on 12 January 1915, the official war establishment of the Cardiff City Battalion, 1,070 rank and file, exclusive of officers, was reached. At seven o' clock that Monday evening the lists were closed and the second Cardiff Pals Battalion was ready to begin training.[12]

A Fergus MacKain postcard that tries to capture the reality of life in the trenches – without showing too many of the horrors.

The Cardiff City Battalion soon left for barracks in Porthcawl. They did not stay long but quickly moved on to Colwyn Bay in North Wales, much to the disapproval of the Cardiff Chamber of Commerce. They were adamant that, by taking the battalion away, it was costing local traders around £20,000 a week.[13] It was not an argument that was likely to sway the military authorities.

After eight months in North Wales, the battalion moved to Winchester along with other units of the 38th (Welsh) Division. They took time to visit Cardiff on the way, parading at the Arms Park before being granted a brief twenty-four-hour leave. It was all too short a respite. At four o'clock on 27 November 1915, the battalion assembled in King Edward VII Avenue, Cathays Park, and entrained for the last time from their home city:

> Instead of the joyous shouts and plaudits which greeted the brave soldiers on the previous day, now there were tears of distress at the parting. Mothers, wives and sweethearts tried to suppress their emotions but it was to no avail. Whilst the troops stood valiantly and stolidly, listening to the farewell address of the Lord Mayor, the women completely broke down.[14]

The battalion embarked for France on 4 December, and served for several months in the Givenchy/Festubert area where they lost about fifty men, including their commanding officer Colonel Gaskell, who died of wounds on 17 May 1915. They then moved to the Somme and took part in the Welsh Division's fateful attack on Mamaetz Wood.

On 7 July the battalion was detailed to take part in the assault on the Hammerhead strongpoint at Mametz, their right flank cruelly exposed to enemy machine-gun fire. The attack left them with approximately 450 casualties, over 150 dead. Among them were the Welsh rugby internationals Dick Thomas and John L. Williams.

Further heavy losses at the Third Battle of Ypres in 1917 decimated what remained of the Cardiff City Battalion, and early in 1918 it was disbanded. However, the real damage had been done eighteen months before when, in the words of one survivor from the Battle of Mametz Wood, 'on the Somme, the Cardiff City Battalion died'.[15]

Sketches of Tommy's life Up the line — Nº 7

One of the bright spots in our life.

Visé Paris 763

One of the bright spots of the day – the regular issue of the rum ration!

4

Three Ports

It was clear that, once Britain entered the war, independent coal exports from places like Cardiff and Penarth would be greatly reduced. There were, of course, significant compensations. The use of coal by the Admiralty and by industry – as well as by Britain's allies – now received priority. Where better to get this vitally needed coal than from South Wales, and where better to ship it from than the three main South Wales ports.

When the price of coal rose from twenty-two to a staggering fifty-five shillings a ton, it was obvious that the coal magnates of Cardiff and the two other ports in the Vale would not be suffering unduly.[1] Neither, it seemed, would the dockers of the Welsh ports, who would at least be assured of work for the duration of the war. For the sailors who took the coal all over the world, even in the early days of 1914 the future seemed much less sure.

On the eve of war, there were 113 coal-exporting businesses in Cardiff and approximately seventy ship-owning firms. It meant that these firms owned and managed about 320 vessels. The largest was the firm of Evan Thomas Radcliffe with twenty-eight ships. John Cory came next with nineteen, while companies like Morel, Reardon Smith and Edward Nicholl each owned ten vessels.[2]

Other firms, many of them operating just a single ship, proliferated. Sometimes these small firms prospered and were able to extend their fleet. So, the Gibbs Company began business with just one vessel, the 3668-ton *South Wales*, employed on the Rio de Janeiro run, like most of the tramp steamers, carrying coal outward, grain inward; by 1915 their fleet had extended to three ships.[3] All three Gibbs vessels, incidentally, were lost during the war.

Despite the war, trade from the South Wales ports was lively in 1914, exceeding all previous years apart from 1913. It was estimated that about 52 million tons of coal had been produced in the South Wales coalfields, regardless of the fact that, out of a workforce of 23,000, approximately 40,000 had joined the Army. Much of the coal mined in the Rhondda and Rhymney Valleys went to the Royal and Merchant Navies.

However, by the end of 1914, the shortage of labour, both in the mines and on the docks, was beginning to cause more than a few problems:

The trouble is a shortage of labour. Men are wanted at the collieries, works, docks, on the railways, and for the steamers that carry Welsh commodities to the distant places of the earth. Some of the best workmen have become soldiers, not in scores but in thousands, and while

Merchant seamen and passengers cling to an upturned lifeboat after their ship is torpedoed – one of many victims in Germany's campaign of unrestricted submarine warfare.

the patriotism of the community has demanded the sacrifice, the business of the country calls for others to fill their places in the industrial army.[4]

On 4 February 1915 Germany declared the waters around Britain and Ireland a war zone. In future her submarines would sink all ships, merchant or naval, encountered in this zone without warning. It was the start of the first phase of unrestricted submarine warfare, and while they had only thirty-seven U-boats, of which only one-third were available for use, between March and May 1915 the Germans sank 115 merchant ships.[5] The furore around the sinking of the *Lusitania* that March caused the German 'sink on sight' campaign to be restricted, at least until 1916 when total war was reintroduced. Nevertheless it remained a difficult time for British merchant ships.

This virtual blockade of the British coast was both chastening and terrifying to a nation used to unhindered control of the sea. *The Western Mail* for 15 March 1915 gave the following bleak and horrifying figures:

The following are the figures since the 'blockade' started –
Merchant vessels sunk – 17
Sunk by submarine -13
Sunk by mines – 1
Sunk by cruisers – 4.
Since the beginning of the war, 47 fishing vessels have been sunk or captured.[6]

The first Cardiff-owned ship to be lost in the war was the *Cornish City*, sunk off the coast of Brazil. A few weeks after that, the German cruiser *Emden* accounted for the Tatem's-owned

Exford, seizing her as a prize. The *Emden* sailed on to destruction at the hands of HMAS *Sydney* off the Cocos Islands.

Several Cardiff tramp steamers were converted into Q-ships, decoy vessels that would lure U-boats to the surface and then attack them with concealed guns. It was a dangerous game to play, as the *Dunraven* – previously owned by Radcliffe's – discovered when she was torpedoed and sunk off the Cornish coast.

Seventeen Cardiff ships were lost in 1915 but that was just the start. The following year thirty-eight went to the bottom. The worst year for Cardiff losses was 1917 when, despite the introduction of a convoy system, 124 ships were sunk. A further thirty-one were lost in 1918, bringing the total number of Cardiff ships sunk in the war to approximately 210.[7]

Cardiff shipowners watched helplessly as their fleets were decimated. Tatem's shipping company, which started the war with seventeen vessels, lost nine of them before the Armistice was eventually signed. Yet for the shipowners it was not the end of the world. They may have lost their vessels and their cargoes but they were handsomely compensated by the government and, consequently, did not lose out.[8]

The sailors, on the other hand, whose pay was stopped the moment their ship was sunk, certainly did. Their war was grindingly hard, and if they survived the sudden torpedo or shell they would probably have to face several days in an open boat before there was any chance of rescue. It was a hard and brutal war, and by the middle of 1916 it was clear things would not be getting any easier.

The *South Wales Echo* for 24 July 1916 reported the loss of three Cardiff ships – the *Llongwen*, *Knutsford* and *President* – and went on to rub salt into the wounds: 'There have been, latterly,

Coal tips at work; thousands of tons were taken on board every day at Cardiff, Penarth and Barry. It was unglamorous work but essential to the war effort.

suggestions in the German papers that the campaign of submarine piracy which threatened a break with the United States should be persisted in, and events of the last few days suggest this course has been adopted.'[9]

Small wonder that in ports like Cardiff, Penarth and Barry, anti-Kaiser emotions ran high: 'The anniversary of the birthday of the Kaiser has passed but the anticipated victories on land and sea, in the air and under the water, have also vanished. To utter the usual good wishes at such a time, of "Many Happy Returns of the Day," seem certainly somewhat incongruous.'[10]

The docks area of Cardiff was the scene of unprecedented dispute – riots might be stretching it a bit far – in July 1916 when 'hundreds of British sailors now in port demonstrated against the employment of Chinese labour on Admiralty transports.'[11]

There had apparently been rumblings and disquiet for several weeks, before the SS *Katanga* of Glasgow docked at Cardiff on 25 July and her all-Chinese crew were paid off. The Chinese sailors immediately went to the Board of Trade offices in the dock in order to resign. British sailors, fearful that they were being overlooked for berths on ships about to leave the port, quickly complained.

At 10.30 a.m. on 26 July a large crowd gathered just opposite the Board of Trade offices, where they made their feelings quite clear. When Mr R. C. Neale, superintendent of the Board of Trade, appeared in front of the crowd and asked how many of them wished to sign on, about 500 hands were raised.

The Admiralty, when contacted by Captain Parker, chief of the Transport Office, was clear that in their mind there was no problem, no reason why the Chinese sailors should not sign on to any ship. This opinion was reached despite the fact that they had received a telegram from Parker stating, 'If steamer 'Katanga' takes Chinese seamen, Union cannot be held responsible for what happens.'[12]

As the morning wore on there were heated moments. Chinese sailors, whenever they were spotted, were hooted and booed, but the union officials managed to keep the British away and there was no violence. Part of the trouble stemmed from an agreement made in October 1915, stating that the Admiralty would not employ Chinese or other nationalities if there were British seamen waiting for berths. That July there were apparently 350 British sailors waiting for employment.

After much argument, the Admiralty finally gave in: 'The SS 'Katanga,' which has been the subject of dispute at Cardiff Docks in regard to the signing on of a Chinese crew, today signed on a British crew, in accordance with Admiralty instructions.'[13]

*

Fear of the enemy was very real in a place like Penarth, whose very existence depended largely on the docks. The significance of the conflict was not lost on the local press either. As early as 5 August they had dubbed it 'The Greatest War in the World's History' – the capital letters being deliberately used to emphasise the point.[14]

Penarth Docks had their peak year, like the other Vale ports, in 1913, with 4.5 million tons of coal being exported. For a relatively small port, that was an incredible figure, one that would take some beating. The outbreak of war put an end to all thoughts of similar returns in 1914 but, even so, the port – with its floating dock or pontoon for repair work – remained hugely popular and important.

The floating dock or pontoon at Penarth. This view shows the SS *Ethelhilda*, the first vessel to be lifted on to the pontoon.

Built by Swan Hunter on the Tyne, the floating dock was 382 feet in length, and had been towed to Penarth in 1909. Capable of dry-docking ships of up to 4,500 tons, it was a very useful facility, particularly during the war years when the need to repair damaged vessels quickly and without fuss was of paramount importance.

At this time the docks had fourteen tips on the south side, four movable ones on the north side of the basin and two movable ones on the north edge of the dock.[15] They were all well used during the four years of conflict.

Penarth Head Fort was fully manned in the early days of the war, despite a degree of opposition from local people who feared that the firing of guns from the fort might cause the fragile cliffs of Penarth Head to crumble and fall. It was a minor irritation, however, as there were greater things for the people of Penarth to worry about: 'Owing to the Admiralty commandeering so many horses from Penarth, several small firms are considering the purchase of motor delivery vans.'[16]

The Dardanelles campaign began in April 1915, and Penarth, relatively safe and secure, was considered an ideal place to prepare transports. Many Penarth merchant seamen were involved in the campaign, most of them serving on supply ships or lying off the Gallipoli Peninsula and then ferrying soldiers ashore onto the landing beaches.

The thought of Gallipoli was not always a comforting one and there were several instances of Penarth sailors refusing to join their ships. In the early stages of the campaign *The Penarth Times* listed five such men. When the time came for their ship to sail, they refused to go on board. By doing so, they seriously delayed the departure of their vessel. Having already signed on, however, the men were guilty of a criminal offence and were duly sentenced to hard labour.[17]

The docks at Penarth saw two sudden deaths at the beginning of 1916. In January, Norwegian sailor Frank Anderson fell from a gangplank, smashing his head on the dock wall before disappearing into the murky depths below. Some reports said that he was returning from shore leave in Penarth and was drunk when he fell.

In February, sixteen-year-old William Morris from Windsor Road was working on the floating dock when he was struck by a stanchion that fell from the ship above. It was the young man's first job and he was inexperienced. Nevertheless he was killed instantly in the freak accident.[18]

The year 1917 brought even more sudden deaths. John Lye was clearly ill when he came ashore from the SS *Peerless* but he refused to see a doctor and took himself off to his home in Penarth. He had been torpedoed twice, firstly being machine-gunned as he and his colleagues sat helplessly in their lifeboat. When sunk for a second time, he spent four days adrift in an open boat before being rescued. On 20 September he collapsed and died at his home. Medical opinion stated that the cause was heart failure after the stress and shock of the torpedoing.[19]

Augustin Richard was not a native of Penarth. He was a French sailor, a crew member of the SS *St Louis*. He died on 8 November 1917 when his leg became caught in a coil of rope as the ship was being moved so that coal could be loaded into its forward hold. Richard's leg was cut off and, despite the assistance of crew members who applied a tourniquet, he died from shock and loss of blood before the doctor arrived.[20]

Merchant seamen from the town continued to run serious risks throughout the war. When the SS *Borgary* was torpedoed and sunk on Christmas Eve 1916, no fewer than seven of her crew came from Penarth. They managed to get into a lifeboat before the *Borgary* sank but then had to spend three days adrift before they were finally picked up by a Norwegian steamer.

James Matthews from the town was a steward on a ship that sailed from Penarth Dock in the early part of 1917. When she was torpedoed, twenty-four of her crew, including the captain, went down with her, but Matthews and eight others were picked up by the U-boat. They were detained on board while the submarine cruised the Western Approaches for a month before finally returning to Germany. Matthews was then sent to the Kriegsgefangenenlager POW camp in Brandenburg, where he spent the rest of the war.[21]

On 8 January 1917 there was a near riot on board a ship loading coal in Penarth Dock. It began with an argument between two or three of the crew members – although the exact cause remains unknown – and escalated from there. The main culprit or perpetrator was a sailor from the Cogan area of the town: 'A Cogan man was implicated in the quarrel, and he was finally overpowered, handcuffed and conveyed to the police station. As the boat was sailing that evening no charge was preferred against the man and he was accordingly marched back to the vessel, still wearing the "bracelets."'[22]

Such episodes were common in all ports. In wartime they were considered especially serious as no ship's captain ever wanted to sail short-handed.

*

If Cardiff and Penarth were busy during the war years, then the tippers, trimmers and dockers from Barry simply never stopped working.

Between 1914 and 1918 Barry Docks were crowded with ships, and dozens of seamen – Lascars, Danes, British, Africans, Norwegians – thronged the streets of the town. With Welsh coal suddenly in great demand thanks to the German successes in the early months of the war, huge amounts of the precious fuel were now exported through the docks at Barry.

Like Cardiff and Penarth, incoming ships were stopped for interrogation and checking before they reached the docks. In the beginning, some of these vessels were reluctant to slow down, their captains refusing to answer the signals to stop engines. On several occasions, the fort at Barry was forced to open fire. One ship had her funnel knocked down, another was hit on the mast. The Belgian ship *Beermngert* took three hits before she finally came to a halt.[23]

On New Year's Eve, 1914, the Greek steamer *Antonias* was issued with repeated requests to stop but ignored them all. The fort opened fire and the ship's Chief Officer was wounded in the leg, hardly good for Anglo–Greek relations but inevitable when war fever was at its height.[24]

British ships crowded the docks but there were many foreign vessels, too – one of the reasons for ships failing to stop when ordered to do so was, quite simply, the crews did not understand the messages. In the days before radio, the miracle was that there were not more incidents.

For a young man, the sight of those crowded docks and row after row of dirty colliers and tramp steamers was nothing short of spectacular:

We never went anywhere in those days. People were born, lived and died in the same town, even the same house. The one trip that sticks in my mind was when I went to Barry in the first few years of the war. I don't know, the end of 1914, perhaps?

My father was a farmer and haulage contractor and he had some business in Barry. I was working on the family farm and he agreed to take me with him. I think it was to keep me quiet. I'd been going on about joining the Merchant Navy or lying about my age – I was only 14 at the time – and enlisting in the army. Anyway, he took me with him. Mind you, he docked me two days' wages. 'It'll pay for your train fare,' he said.

We went up on the train from Pembroke Dock early in the morning. It took five or six hours, I think. Into Cardiff, then out to Barry. We stayed the night in a boarding house on the main road. Holton Street [*sic*, Holton Road], I think it was.

Next day, father did his business and I wandered round the town and Docks. I'd never seen so many ships. And remember, I was used to seeing ships in Milford Haven but it was nothing like this. Colliers, tramps, sailing ships, big steamers, you name it and it was there. They were moored side by side, right across the Dock. You couldn't see the water, there were so many of them. To a young lad like me it was magical. Within a day or so those ships would be off, around the world, visiting places I could only dream about.

And the smoke, it was everywhere, like a low cloud across the town. The noise? I can't describe it. It was like – like a thunderstorm. Metal was clashing against metal. People were shouting. It was a real hive of activity. The place was alive.

Then father finished his business and we were back on the train. Back to sleepy old Pembroke again.[25]

SOUVENIR
DE
GLORIEUSE
MEMOIRE

1914   1915

Best Wishes for a Happy Future

The government was always eager to stress the concept of unity – unity with Allies and internal unity within the country. In fact, tempers were often frayed and, on many occasions, open warfare seemed likely.

The port of Barry was a rough, tough place. Sailors brought ready money – and a will to spend it – and the pubs of the town did a roaring trade, as did the 'ladies of the night', a feature in every port in the land. Add in a healthy proportion of Belgian refugees, the painter Emile Claus among them (he lodged in a house in Porthkerry Park), and you had a melting pot of immense proportions.

Anti-German sentiment was rife all over Britain in the early part of the war, but in May 1915 it even affected work at Barry Docks: 'In May about 150 tippers and coal trimmers on the Docks ceased work as a protest against the employment of naturalised Germans. They declined upon any terms to resume work for a couple of hours.'[26]

It was inevitable, with such frantic use of the port facilities, that accidents would happen. The *Penarth Advertiser* for 8 June 1915 reported on one such event in Barry Dock:

On Friday night a fire of an extraordinary and destructive character broke out at Barry, causing damage to the extent of £5000 or £6000. A few weeks ago after a fire on board the Norwegian steamer 'Vinster,' lying at No. 2 Dock, a cargo of coconut or copra was discharged and stocked on a large open tract of land running alongside the dockside.

It is presumed that owing to the excessive heat of the past few days this material, representing about 75,000 bags, caught fire and rapidly spread over its whole area. Vast volumes of smoke extending over several acres preceded huge tongues of flames, giving a lurid hue to the sky which was visible for many miles.

The overpowering heat stultified the efforts of the combined fire brigades to extinguish the flames, and their engines were directed on the preservation of the adjoining property, and the prevention of the fire spreading. Many thousands of tons of pit props were removed from the danger zone. The hasty departure of hundreds of rabbits and rats 'to pastures new' caused an amusing diversion to the onlookers.[27]

It is easy to imagine the feature writer of the *Penarth Advertiser*, a paper more used to running adverts for furniture dealers and the local cinemas than reporting the news, licking his lips and sharpening his adjectival clauses at the prospect of such a juicy story.

Merchant Navy sailors from Barry, like those from Cardiff and Penarth, put their lives at risk every time they sailed out of the port. In all, some 279 Barry Merchant Navy sailors lost their lives in the war, their names now recorded on the memorial in front of the civic offices in the town. Barry men served in the Royal Navy as well.

Signalman Charles Kirkby died on the *Defence* when she was sunk at the Battle of Jutland, blown to pieces by the guns of Admiral Hipper's battlecruisers. Admiral Arbuthnot and 903 men went down alongside Kirkby, a death toll that included another Barry man, Able Seaman Walter Down.

The Battle of Jutland, the only time the battle fleets of Britain and Germany ever met in combat, saw the deaths of Stoker Alfred John Harvey from Cadoxton, Able Seaman Robert Davies and Engine Room Artificer Thomas Phillips, all killed when the battlecruisers *Indefatigable* and *Invincible* were destroyed.[28] Admiral Beatty's famous comment – 'There's something wrong with our bloody ships today' – does not begin to catch the pain and sorrow of the Barry families of these unfortunate men.

A few years later Able Seaman W. H. Rees was drowned when the cruiser *Hampshire* struck a mine and sank off Orkney. Field Marshal Lord Kitchener, the man who had raised the Pals battalions went down with the ship, on his way to a meeting in Russia.

Accidents in the docks were inevitable. At the end of January 1918 a Norwegian steamer, the SS *Hassel*, was in the process of docking when she collided with the Newport pilot cutter. The pilot cutter, carrying three pilots and three assistant pilots, quickly sank, but boats from the shore were soon on the scene and pulled the men to safety.[29]

Just before the Armistice in 1918, the SS *Hedley* was waiting to sail. In the early hours of 5 October she lurched to one side and turned turtle. The crew managed to scramble to safety, but poorly loaded coal had caused the instability – a clear case of less haste, more speed.[30]

It was later estimated that 8,000 men from Barry enlisted in the Army and Royal Navy during the war. Many of these were caught up in the forced enlistment or conscription that came after 1916, but many more were volunteers who joined up in the early stages. About 2,000 more Barry men served in the Merchant Marine. As one paper put it, 'In almost incredible short time the streets and workshops were gleaned of the flower of its manhood.'[31]

5

A Pier at War

Penarth Pier had been the central focus of the town for twenty years before war broke out. Each summer thousands of visitors had flocked to promenade upon the wooden decking, where they could enjoy the sensation of being at sea but without feeling seasick. Now, that pier was to find itself as an important weapon in time of war.

The advantage of the pier as a base for searchlights, low lying and flat to the water, was recognised by the authorities from the first few days of the conflict and, as we have seen, a searchlight was quickly positioned on the seaward end.

Realising its value, however, the military wanted more than just one searchlight, and consequently Penarth Pier was soon requisitioned by the Army. The Pier Company, like the owners of railway lines and coal mines across the country, had little say in the matter. The pier would be controlled by the Army for the duration of the war.

It was a fairly harmonious arrangement – the Army got the pier but the public was still allowed to use it, provided they did not interfere with the workings of the military minds or distract the soldiers as they went about their work.

The Royal Engineers who had set up the first searchlight on the pier quickly settled down to man it. They worked in conjunction with a detachment of Royal Garrison Artillery, complete with two field guns, that was stationed on the cliffs above the seafront.

By 1916 the officer in charge of the Royal Engineers was Lieutenant Christopher John Evans. His wife and daughter Florence were with him in Penarth:

> My father was a professional soldier. He had been a Regimental Sergeant Major but he was commissioned as an officer when war broke out and then posted to take command of the searchlight battery in Penarth. He had his office at the seaward end of the Pier, next to the old pavilion where they used to hold concerts before the war. The men were mostly billeted in shops along the Esplanade but some were under canvas, in tents on the rough ground next to the Yacht Club.
>
> The REs had a mascot, a black and white terrier called Tiger. He used to run up and down the Pier, totally unconcerned that there was a sheer drop on either side of him. But then, in 1917, the REs moved up onto Penarth Head, on top of the cliff. Poor Tiger carried on charging about, his usual playful ways – until one day he became too excited and charged over the cliff edge. Head first, down he went, and of course he was killed instantly.[1]

Penarth Pier, surely the most unusual item ever requisitioned by the military in time of war.

The old pavilion, the Bijou Pavilion as it was known, was closed during the first few months of the war, but summer was dying anyway and there was little or no immediate call for shows and other entertainments. Some of the pier shops remained open, including the cafés, and provided the public could pay their entrance fee – the pier was privately run in those days – people were allowed to wander up and down and enjoy what amenities remained open. Florence Evans recalled,

> I remember playing on a football machine on the Pier. It was one of those games where the players were fixed onto long horizontal poles and you spun the handles to get them to kick the ball. If you gave the machine a good, hard push then the money you'd put in to play the game fell back out. It didn't always work but when it did it was great because you got an extra game for nothing.
>
> After a while they opened up the Pavilion again. I can remember the soldiers in my father's unit putting on shows for the people of Penarth. I had to sell the programmes, something that I quite enjoyed. And then, sometimes, the amateur theatre companies in Penarth would put on shows for the soldiers. All good fun. I think the soldiers and the people of Penarth got on very well with each other at that stage. At least there was no trouble, as far as I can remember.[2]

When, at the end of 1916, professional singers and actors were employed again, the prospect of regular shows returning to the Bijou Pavilion was an alluring one. Alfred Newton, who had run the pre-war shows in Penarth, returned to manage the pier entertainments, offering matinees at 3.15 and evening shows at 8.00 p.m. In April 1917 Mr Will Game and his concert party 'Pierrot Pierette and Piano' were in residence and were playing to packed houses.[3] The people of Penarth had been without such entertainment for far too long: 'On Saturday last many patrons were unable to secure seats, nearly 300 seats having been booked in advance for the evening … the bookings have been so heavy for the last few Saturdays that they have been almost beyond the possibilities of a somewhat depleted staff to cope with.'[4]

In 1917 the Army decided to build special searchlight platforms at the foot of Penarth Head, half a mile away from the pier – the move that spelled the demise of the unfortunate

The searchlight platforms built for the Royal Engineers. This post-war shot shows them intact at the foot of the cliff – the steps leading up the cliff can just be seen. In the background the beginnings of Cardiff Docks can be glimpsed.

Tiger. The platforms were reached by a set of near-vertical steps leading up and down the cliff face. They were rickety and downright dangerous, particularly on windy nights, but somehow the steps and platforms survived until they were destroyed by a cliff fall in the 1960s.

Penarth Pier never saw a gun fired in anger but there were quite severe consequences of the Army's occupation. Despite moving onto the purpose-built platforms on Penarth Head, the pier was not decommissioned and returned to the Pier Company until after the Armistice was signed. When that was finally done, it quickly became clear that the structure had suffered considerable damage during its years of war service.

After assessing the damage, the Pier Company put in a claim for £7,228 to the War Compensation Court. They were awarded the sum of just £353. *The Penarth News*, naturally somewhat partial in its opinion, commented, 'Nobody can justify the absurd award of the War Compensation Court … It is an ill reward for war service, and wretchedly unjust to the people who have to bear the financial burden.'[5]

The award of £353 against a claim of £7,228 would be laughable if it were not so unjust. The trouble was, most of the damage was to the landing stage at the seaward end of the pier, caused through poor maintenance during the war years rather than wilful damage or even accident. Made of greenheart timber, the pontoon required constant careful attention and, with Piermaster Leonard and most of his staff away serving in the Navy, the Pier Company had neglected to maintain it.

Florence Evans remembers that her father, Lieutenant Evans, was one of the main witnesses called to give evidence at the Court:

> The Pier Company claimed that the damage to the Pier had been caused by soldiers wearing their heavy army boots on the decking. Those boots, they said, had caused damage to the wood and that was why they wanted compensation.
>
> My father gave evidence and was able to show that no soldiers ever wore boots on the Pier. He had written orders, orders that he still had in his possession and that he showed to the Court. They were orders from the War Department, stating that whenever soldiers went onto the Pier they had to remove their boots and wear plimsoles instead. That evidence was what made the Court give its verdict and offer such a small amount of compensation.

When I'm talking now, I can still remember those plimsoles that the men wore. I thought they looked so funny, white plimsoles with pink or red soles, and army uniforms. In a way it was quite sad because the Pier Company felt it had done its duty but my father felt the same way, only for the other side. If he'd have ignored his orders it would have looked bad on him.[6]

Despite the matter being raised in parliament, Stanley Baldwin, Chancellor of the Exchequer, refused to listen to any appeal, and the judgement stood. It caused more than a little bad feeling in Penarth, putting rather a sour note to the good relations between the soldiers and the local people. As one local paper commented, 'Without doubt, more would have been paid for commandeering a fried fish shop in a back street.'[7]

*

It was not just Penarth Pier that was requisitioned. The trawlers of the Cardiff fishing fleet Neale and West were taken over by the Admiralty, the tiny trawlers and drifters being quickly armed with a single gun and converted into minesweepers.

The paddle steamers of the White Funnel Fleet, small ships that had been offering pleasure cruises from places like Penarth and Barry for many years, also found themselves called up for service. With their shallow draught and flat bottoms, the paddlers were ideal for use as patrol vessels and, in particular, as minesweepers.

Between August 1914 and July 1915, ten of these ships were taken into naval service. The *Devonia* and *Brighton Queen* went first, leaving for war service on 30 September 1914. Then, in early December, four more – the *Cambria*, *Westward Ho*, *Glen Avon* and *Lady Ismay* – joined the ranks of the Royal Navy. They gathered together, initially at least, at the pier in Barry: 'Four of the fleet of passenger steamers belonging to Messrs P & A Campbell Ltd, which ply in the summer months on passenger service in the Bristol Channel, arrived at Barry pontoon yesterday. The steamers have been armed and will be used for patrol purposes by the Admiralty.'[8]

Together with the *Devonia* and *Brighton Queen*, these tiny ships made up the Grimsby minesweeping fleet. In the summer of 1915 they cleared mines prior to the bombardment of Zeebrugge, and regularly patrolled the North Sea. Then, on 6 October 1915 off Nieuwpoort, the *Brighton Queen* struck a mine and was sunk, taking seven sailors down with her.

She was not to be the only paddle steamer lost in the war. The *Lady Ismay* also hit a mine and was sunk in December 1915, before the fleet was re-stationed on the Tyne. They remained there from 1917 until peace was declared. Two other paddlers, the *Britannia* and the *Glen Usk*, served on the Clyde, the *Glen Usk* taking a party of Scottish schoolchildren to watch the surrender of the German High Seas Fleet at Scapa Flow in November 1918.[9]

The *Ravenswood* and *Albion* were stationed at Dover, having been requisitioned in July 1915. They were part of the famous Dover Patrol, serving alongside destroyers, like the *Broke*, and huge, big gun monitors. They were involved in sweeping mines during the St George's Day raid on the submarine bases at Zeebrugge and Ostend in 1918, and were returned to the P. & A. Campbell firm in the early part of the following year.

By the final days of 1916, only the *Waverley* and the *Glen Rosa* remained to ply their trade – a grossly restricted trade – around the Bristol Channel. Even this came to an end when the final

The guns of 1914 ended cruising on the Bristol Channel. It was hardly the time for such fripperies – and, besides, the Admiralty had other plans for the paddle steamers.

The paddle steamer *Glen Avon* in her wartime colours. She was one of the first paddlers to be called up for war service, and served as a minesweeper for four long years.

two paddlers were 'called up' in May 1917. That left only the ancient *Duchess of Devonshire*, hastily brought out of retirement to make a regular ferry run between Cardiff and Weston.[10]

Out of all the White Funnel paddle steamers, the *Barry* had by far the most adventurous and, arguably, the most dangerous war, being heavily involved in the disastrous and ill-conceived Dardanelles Campaign.

Arriving at Mudros in August 1915 – it is hard to imagine how difficult the voyage of this flat-bottomed, shallow-draught paddler must have been across the Bay of Biscay and in to the Mediterranean – she was soon operating off the beaches of Gallipoli, ferrying troops ashore to Suvla Bay, Anzac Cove and other places.

In December she was again busy off the beaches, this time evacuating the luckless and unfortunate soldiers after a pointless and particularly bloody episode in British military history. The *Barry* did not return to Britain after Gallipoli, and was later present during the landings at Salonika; it is interesting to wonder if any of the Cardiff Pals recognised the paddle steamer that used to take them on summer cruises around the Bristol Channel.

The *Barry* spent the rest of the war in the Middle East and only returned to civilian duties in September 1919.

6

Vale Soldiers at War

While the Royal and Merchant Navies took many men from the Vale of Glamorgan – and from towns and cities like Barry and Cardiff – the vast majority of those who enlisted chose to serve in the Army. That was where the pressing need lay.

Many of these men joined up in the first two or three months of the war when, in Britain as a whole, 33,204 men took the King's shilling. The age limit for volunteers was originally eighteen to thirty-one, but such was the outcry in the country, with every man seemingly wanting to enlist, that the upper limit was soon extended to thirty-five for men without any previous military experience.[1]

It could not last, of course. Anyone with foresight could see that once the war fever began to ebb, once people realised things would not be 'over by Christmas', enlistment figures would drop away.

Although Britain had always relied on her sea power to keep the country safe, as the conflict developed it became increasingly clear that the Western Front was where the war would be won or lost. Thousands more men would be needed before that could possibly happen. With enlistment falling rapidly, how to procure those men was a serious problem for those in authority.

The Military Service Bill, a limited system of conscription, was introduced in January 1916 in an attempt to boost this flagging recruitment. The flow of volunteers had never totally died away, but it had certainly thinned out after the hysteria of August 1914. The system of partial conscription did little to fill the gap and, consequently, full conscription finally came into operation in April 1916. Those men from the Vale who had not joined up now found they had no choice, and the military machine soon gathered them into its grasp.

What the soldiers, volunteers and conscripts found when they eventually reached the front line was vastly different from what they had expected. Trenches were little better than holes scraped out of the earth, and the biggest battle was not against the Germans but against the mud and water that seemed to drain constantly into the British quarters: 'It seemed that our superiors did not inwardly admit that comfort was desirable … the true British spirit of waging war was to scorn any perfectioning [*sic*] of our present position because we would, in a day or so, according to the theory, be driving the enemy out of his trenches.'[2]

Death was ever present and it was not long before the papers in Cardiff and the Vale were recording casualties. Sometimes those casualties were men who had occupied lofty positions

The first contingent of volunteers from Cowbridge line up for photographs on Cowbridge station. Several of these men would never return to their sleepy Vale community.

in society, men who everybody thought were untouchable. The *Penarth Advertiser* had it about right when it recorded one particular death in action:

> Death is no respecter of persons, and on the battlefield high and low, rich and poor share the same risks. We regret to announce the death of the Hon Archer Windsor-Clive, second son of the Earl and Countess of Plymouth, who died from wounds received at the Battle of Mons. He was only 24 years of age and a brilliant future apparently lay before him, but duty called and, along with his regiment, the Coldstream Guards, he manfully took his part, and like a hero fell.[3]

There were small compensations, however – things like the Christmas Day Truce of 1914, which has been well recorded and often written about. Suffice to say that many Vale men were there in the trenches when the event occurred. Many of them wrote home about it, as this graphic and vibrant account from the *South Wales Echo* shows:

> From our trenches – 'Good morning, Fritz.' No answer. 'Good morning, Fritz.' (Still no answer.) 'GOOD MORNING FRITZ!'
> From the German trenches – 'Good morning.'
> From our trench – 'How are you?'
> 'All right.'
> 'Come over here, Fritz.'
> 'No. If I come I get shot.'
> 'No you won't, come on.'
> 'No fear.'
> 'Come and get some fags, Fritz.'
> 'No, you come half way and I meet you.'
> 'All right.'

One of our fellows thereupon filled his pockets with fags and got over the trench. The German got over his trench; and right enough, they met half way and shook hands, Fritz taking the fags and giving chocolate in exchange.[4]

Other accounts indicate that the unofficial truce was begun by the Germans. The singing of Christmas carols occurred throughout the trenches and, in some sections, men did meet in No Man's Land to exchange gifts. It all depended on which part of the front line you were serving in. Wyn Griffith wrote about a plan to keep the peace all day long, of creating a situation where there would be no rifle fire at night and a football game in the afternoon. In his case, though, it came to nothing:

An irate Brigadier came spluttering up the line, thundering hard, throwing a 'court martial' into every other sentence, ordering an extra dose of military action that night, and breathing fire everywhere. We had evidently jeopardized the safety of the Allied cause. I suspect that across No Man's Land a similar scene was being played, for later in the day the guns became active.[5]

Private Frank Pope from Penarth – later to become a casualty of war – wrote home about his experiences during that Christmas period. For him it was New Year rather than Christmas Day that stuck in the memory:

Christmas in the trenches, a silk postcard of the type that was hugely popular with the soldiers, and made, usually in a form of cottage industry, by the French and Belgian women.

We were exchanging greetings with the Germans on Xmas morning and at midnight on New Year's Eve we could hear them singing and cheering, with their band playing all the time … at twelve-o-clock we started as well. We were singing to them and they to us. The Germans have got 'Tipperary' off to a treat. Then we finished up with singing the old year out and the new year in but instead of bells we had our rifles.[6]

The Christmas Truce obviously only applied to men in the front line. If your unit was out resting, or in reserve, it had little or no effect on you. That did not stop one Barry man, Percy E. Thomas, enjoying the Christmas festivities: 'We went out on Christmas Eve and shot a pig. So on the following day we had a really good dinner of roast pork and vegetables, finishing up with pudding. We didn't half enjoy ourselves.'[7]

Private Thomas did not say where he and his comrades found the pig but, as farmers often remained close up to the lines – at least until the violence of the Second Battle of Ypres drove them away – it is likely to have been stolen or purloined from some unfortunate Belgian smallholder.

Christmas was one thing, fighting the war was something entirely different. In 1915, with forced conscription looming, Cardiff City Corporation gave the government the names of 2,000 employees then working for them. Lord Kitchener had recently asked that skilled craftsmen, tradesmen and engineers who had previously been in 'reserved occupations' be released for munitions work – running the war, it seemed, was more important than running the city's tramcar system.

A letter in the 16 March 1915 issue of the *Western Mail* sheds an interesting light on medical science of the day. Before the war, Surgeon Lieutenant W. Rogers, attached to the Cheshire

The Christmas Day Truce of 1914. This shows British and German soldiers gathered together – a little hesitantly, perhaps – in the middle of No Man's Land.

Regiment, had worked at the Barry Town accident hospital. In March 1915 he felt moved to write to the paper about what he perceived was a pressing need: 'Tommy wants cigarettes, always cigarettes and more of them … Life is hard enough for soldiers at the best of times in war days, and if a few cigarettes can brighten their burden, I think those at home should do their utmost to see that Tommy gets them.'[8]

No mention of the evils of nicotine there, you notice; Lt Rogers was clearly more concerned about the emotional well-being of his charges. He was not alone. The *Weekly Dispatch* newspaper actually ran a 'Smokes for Tommy Campaign' that brought in nearly £300,000 to buy cigarettes for the troops!

The other requirement, it seemed, was a musical one:

Materially, our soldiers want for nothing which it is possible to give them in the circumstances. Morally, they are in very good heart and contented. But there is one thing which nearly all of them refer to when asked, and that is the lack of means of 'making a cheerful noise,' or in other words the dearth of mouth organs.[9]

On 22 April 1915 the Germans launched an offensive that became known as the Second Battle of Ypres. Its original intention was simply to test the strength of British and French defences around the Ypres Salient but the success of the initial assault prompted the Germans to probe deeper.

At sunset on 22nd, French troops saw a greenish mist slowly creeping towards them, and very soon afterwards they began to cough and choke. It was not the first time that the Germans had used chlorine gas – that had already happened on the Eastern Front – but this was its first use in the West and was an altogether more significant and serious development. The poisonous gas was also used against British troops, and thousands of soldiers fled in disarray. A 4-mile gap had been opened in the Allied lines.

War in the trenches, grindingly hard and cruel.

The gap was soon closed, a counter-attack by British and Canadian soldiers halting the German advance. However, a new weapon of war had been employed, and troops, with no gas masks to protect them, had to cope with it as best they could. Gunner Daniel Harries from Barry recalled,

> We were forced back by the horrible poisonous gasses, just as the Canadians were … We were gasping for breath, fairly choked up. I shall never forget that day in a hurry. The gas fumes are terrible … We had to keep putting wet rags on our mouths. You ought to see our poor chaps coming from the trenches, gasping for breath, foaming at the mouth and hardly able to stagger along.[10]

The Allies quickly retaliated with their own brand of poisonous gas. It was first used during the Battle of Loos on 25 September 1915, not totally successfully, as a change in wind direction caused the chlorine gas to blow back into the British trenches. William Willment from Cowbridge (although he was actually born in nearby Llantwit Major) was killed when

British soldiers, wounded and gassed in the attacks at Ypres in 1915. Gas masks were in their infancy, and soldiers had to take what precautions they could. Many of them urinated on sacks or handkerchiefs and wound them around their faces as a way of keeping the gas away.

advancing with the second wave of the attack – over 2,000 men killed and not an inch of enemy ground captured.[11]

The youngest Barry soldier to die in the war was Joseph Burke, just fifteen years old when he passed away at his home in George Street, Barry. In total contrast, the oldest Barry man to die was a sailor, Thomas Williams, the sixty-six-year-old second engineer on the SS *Argus*, sunk in a collision off Norway on 21 October 1917. He and the rest of the crew drowned in the freezing waters.

Three Barry men won the DSO during the war – 2nd Lt Reginald Jones, Major Evan Thomas Rees and William Cooke of the Royal Navy. Cardiff and Penarth each had two Victoria Cross winners, although technically one of the Penarth men came from the village of Sully and one Cardiff winner of the medal was from Milford Haven.

Medals and awards were given out quite liberally, particularly those like the Military Medal, which did not have a pension or gratuity attached to the award, the military authorities being parsimonious and abstemious to the end.

One of the unsung heroes of the war was Cardiff sailor Mr J. Watson, the Master of the *Lady Plymouth*. His award did not even come from the British government, it was actually presented by the French:

> The Board of Trade have received, through the Admiralty, a gold medal and diploma which have been awarded by the French government to Mr J Watson, Master of the steamship 'Lady Plymouth' of Cardiff, in recognition of his services to the French ship 'Calvados,' which was torpedoed in the Mediterranean.[12]

*

Letters from serving soldiers during this war, both to family and friends and to the local papers of Cardiff and the Vale, often contain poems – possibly not great poetry but certainly indicative both of the events and of the emotion of the times.

The First World War was the world's first 'literate' war, Forster's Education Act of 1870 having made education compulsory in Britain. By 1914 almost all of the participants could read and write – something which had happened in almost no previous conflicts, in which battles were fought by men on the edges of society who had, as like as not, enlisted only to escape the poverty trap or as an alternative to prison.

The First World War of 1914–18 was a war fought largely by volunteers. These men had been schooled in an educational system that was in its infancy. It was a system that had done little more than ape the socially superior, long-established public schools of Britain; the people it produced may not have been well grounded in science and technology, but they could remember and recite Tennyson and Wordsworth. More than that, they didn't just read poetry or verse, they wrote it.

As early as the end of August 1914, the *South Wales Echo* had realised the potential that lay in the work of the country's 'soldier-poets' and was eager to publish their efforts: 'The *South Wales Echo* would be pleased to receive, for publication, letters and poems written by those at the front to relatives and friends at home.'[13]

Over the next few months the *Echo*, like all the other papers from the Vale, was inundated with poetry. Much of it was sentimental, almost all was intensely patriotic:

> In a dirty ditch I'm lying, midst
> The dying and the dead
> With a piece of shrapnel sticking in
> My dazed and aching head.
>
> For I've been sorely stricken
> In the carnage that befell
> Among the Seaforth Highlanders
> That day at Neuve Chapel.[14]

The above lines are part of a longer poem written by Private A. T. Rixon, a serving soldier from Penarth, one of the original Old Contemptibles. It is a traditional piece of narrative poetry full of martial glory, but soon, as the horrors of war began to hit home, the mood of the soldier-poets began to change. For Welshman Private Ivor Morgan, about to take ship for Salonika, the atmosphere was full of bad omens, the ineptitude of poor staff work and the inadequacy of those in command:

> What's in the air? Oh, strategic plans
> And banquets for men in corned beef cans.
> Oh yes, there's fever and dread disease,
> Mosquitoes, bluebottles, lice and fleas.[15]

Sometimes, the letters from soldiers were understated and, as a consequence, are far more powerful than any of the horrors they could have described. Sometimes their experiences were so brutal and vivid that they demanded the immediacy of hard, powerful prose. Occasionally, there is an interesting blend of the two:

I have had the most exciting time I have ever had in my life: it was so exciting that half of us were more fit for a lunatic asylum than anywhere else when we came out of the business … [It was] thrilling to see the horses race up with limber shells, with the enemy shells bursting all around them, to see the stretcher bearers carrying the wounded. Of course, sometimes a shell would blow the bearers and stretchers to atoms … They finished shelling us just about dusk with some sort of gas shells that nearly suffocated us, causing us to cough so much that we could hardly put on our respirators. There we were, after dark, with everything in confusion, running blindly about, trying to find some sort of shelter from the shells.[16]

'Exciting' and 'thrilling'? Typical of the time, perhaps, but they are hardly the words most of us would use to describe the experience.

The disasters of the Battle of the Somme brought a degree of cynicism from the men in the trenches and, at least until the government realised that it was counterproductive to allow such thoughts to appear in print, the newspapers continued to publish the poems and stories:

Often in a trench I think
Of those poor chaps at home;
Of perils that surround them
Wherever they may roam.

The train and train collisions,
The Juggernaut motor cars,
Bacteria from cow's milk
And Zeppelins from afar.

How awful it must be at night
To lie in a feather bed;
To find for breakfast when you rise
Butter on your bread.

With all these shocking worries
A man's life must be sad;
And to think that I am missing them
Makes me exceeding glad.

Written by Private C. Maunder of Penarth – later to die in combat – the above poem was published in the *Penarth Times*. Perhaps the editor thought Maunder's words might encourage enlistment, a reasonable enough supposition when you read the poem's final verses:

So to the chaps in old Penarth
I send my sympathy
And ask them, for their safety,
To come out here with me.

I am only a Penarth boy
But I hope some day to see
Some of the boys from old Penarth
In the trenches here with me.[17]

Some of the most effective poems by serving soldiers, men who were not really poets in the way that Sassoon and Wilfred Owen were poets, can be found in descriptions of the conditions they had to endure when going about their daily lives, rather than in recreations of the horrors of battle.

Sergeant H. Marshman from Barry served in Mesopotamia, and produced a classic poem of this type.

The poem, entitled 'The Land of the Ancient Kings', is heartfelt and surprisingly competent, the writer – just an ordinary man from the Barry Dock area – having a good grasp of rhythm and of devices such as internal rhyme:

Have you ever thirsted wildly
For the drink that is not there?
Have you ever seen
A dusky Queen
At dawn, bind up her hair?
When rivers rush on madly,
When their foaming echo rings,
Where the Arabs dwell;
I've named it Hell,
The Land of the Ancient Kings.

I dream I am back in Blighty,
Midst the wintry ice and snow;
And my skates they grate
As I cut an eight
And my blood is all aglow.
But dawn is slowly breaking,
With it a new day brings.
Once more I rise
And curse the flies
In the Land of the Ancient Kings.

Once more at the call of duty
Down the hot road I go.
My clothes they stick,
The dust is thick,
My boots are white as snow;
Of all the fighting frontiers
Where steel on steel still rings,
For broiling heat
You cannot beat
The Land of the Ancient Kings.[18]

The men who sent their poems to the *Barry Dock News*, the *Western Mail*, *Penarth Times* or *South Wales Echo* had few pretensions about their art. They knew they were not poets but they had something to say, a point to make, and at that particular moment in time verse seemed the most effective way of doing it.

*

A large number of men from Penarth and the Vale served with 113th Battery, Royal Garrison Artillery, a unit that had its base at Lavernock along the coast from Penarth.

The 113th Battery was a territorial unit and most of the men had joined long before the guns of August 1914 brought harsh reality to sleepy South Wales. Regular attendance at the weekly parades meant a little extra pocket money and, more importantly, it gave men the chance to enjoy activities with their mates – an extension of the local football, rugby and cricket teams.

The battery was probably the closest thing Penarth ever had to a Pals Battalion, and it was with high spirits that the men embarked for France on 12 June 1916. They arrived just in time to take part in the bloodbath that was the Battle of the Somme.

Gunner Jack Spear from Penarth kept a diary of his time with the battery, his entry for Wednesday 20 June laconically announcing, 'First shell fired by the 113th Siege Battery.' A few days later, during the huge artillery bombardment that proceeded the battle, he wrote, 'German shrapnel was bursting around us for a quarter of an hour. Shell holes all around. The Battery had gas helmets on – 11.45 p.m. a sudden attack of gas and weeping shells.'[19]

Over forty Penarth men were killed in the Battle of the Somme, three of them in the suicidal 'walk' across No Man's Land on the first day. Two brothers from the town were Leonard and Arthur Tregaskis who returned from Canada to enlist in the Cardiff City Pals Battalion. They were killed on the same day, during the attack on Mametz Wood, and now lie buried side by side in the cemetery at Flat Iron Copse.

Jack Spear, in his diary, wrote one account of manning a forward observation post during the great battle:

Sniper bullets came very near our heads whenever we looked over … At 7.45 p.m. our guns went all out. It was like Hell let loose as the boys went over. But as soon as our bombardment started, Fritz started on our trench with machine guns and 4.2 and 5.9 high explosives, giving us a very hot time, making us run and find a good sap. The strafe lasted about an hour and a half.[20]

Sergeant John Regan, a noted sportsman from Penarth who played for the Penarth Thistle Rugby Team, died when a piece of shrapnel struck him in the heart. His fellow sergeant, Tom Bartlett from 113th Battery, wrote a letter of commiseration to Regan's wife, little knowing that within a few days he, too, would be dead: 'It appears that he, with others, was taking cover in a dugout as the enemy were sending over a few shells, one of which smashed the dugout they were in, killing them all.'[21]

Bartlett was buried in the same cemetery as his friend John Regan.

7

Heroes and Villains, Vale Personalities at War

People have always responded to their experiences of war in a variety of different ways. And the Vale of Glamorgan certainly produced its share of heroes and villains.

Lord Ninian, Edward Crighton-Stuart, the third son of the Marquess of Bute, was one of the first of Cardiff's dignitaries to become involved. Since 1910 he had been a Conservative MP for Cardiff, and was the officer commanding the 6th Battalion (Territorials) of the Welsh Regiment. A tactful and caring man, Lord Ninian was unusual among senior officers at the time in that his primary concern was always for the care of his men.

The battalion had been intended for India but orders were changed, and Lord Ninian and his men soon found themselves on the Western Front. In October 1915 the battalion played a significant part in the opening stages of the Battle of Loos but on the second day of a wretchedly misguided and directed assault, they found themselves cut off and in danger of annihilation. During the deepening of entrenchments to protect the men, Lord Ninian took a look over the parapet to check the work and was spotted by a sniper. He was shot in the head and killed.[1] He was one of six Members of Parliament to die in the war.

Cardiff's first Victoria Cross winner of the war was Company Sergeant Major Fred Barter. When war broke out, Barter was a Reservist but, like all time-expired men, he was recalled to his regiment and was soon serving as a CSM in France. He won his VC at Festubert on 16 May 1915 when he led a group of just eight men to capture three German officers, over 100 soldiers and 500 yards of enemy trenches.

When Barter arrived at his home in the Cathays area of Cardiff to enjoy a well-earned rest – and, of course, to garner further publicity and promote enlistment – the response of the public shocked even those in authority:

When Sergeant Major Fred Barter … arrived home on July 5th for seven days well-earned leave, the only apparent blemish on his soldierly frame was a grazed nose, part of the skin of which was missing. It was a disfigurement for which the Boche could take no credit. For off CSM Barter's nose had ricocheted no enemy bullet – only a badly aimed box of chocolates, thrown by an admiring young lady among the thousands who turned out to meet him and welcome him back to his home town.[2]

Above left: The statue of Lord Ninian Stuart, MP and commanding officer of the 6th Battalion, the Welsh Regiment, killed at the Battle of Loos in October 1915. The statue was commissioned from Goscombe John and now stands in Cathays Park in the centre of Cardiff.

Above right: CSM Fred Barter (on the left), Cardiff's first Victoria Cross winner of the war. The other VC winner on the card is Sgt Fuller from Swansea.

Barter was met at the station and driven, along with the Lord Mayor and other civic dignitaries, through crowded streets to City Hall where over 10,000 people were waiting to hear him speak. Barter went on to make more speeches all week, constantly appealing for recruits.

A few weeks later, Fred Barter was given a commission and, as lieutenant, he went back to the trenches. He later transferred to the Indian Army, won the Military Cross during an action in Palestine and retired from the Army in 1922. During the Second World War he served as a major in the Middlesex Home Guard.

The Earl of Dunraven, the man who was lucky not to lose his hair at the Battle of Little Bighorn, was too old to bear arms when the First World War broke out. He had been born in Ireland in 1841 and, as a war correspondent, had covered conflicts such as the Franco-Prussian War of 1870. After serving in the Boer War, the earl had settled down to a quiet life at Dunraven Castle in the Vale of Glamorgan, playing golf at Southerndown and sailing around the world on his yacht *Valkyrie*.

When war broke out, this energetic and dynamic seventy-three-year-old immediately travelled to Bristol where he bought a 400-ton steam yacht, the *Grianaig*. He converted her into a floating hospital and used her to bring wounded soldiers back from France to Britain. In 1915 he took his yacht to Gallipoli where he transported casualties across the Mediterranean to Malta.

Lord Dunraven was nothing if not caustic in his comments about the lack of care offered to wounded soldiers. Perhaps that was one of the reasons why, after the war, he was refused compensation for the money he had spent – a large slice of the family fortune. He was refused simply on the grounds that, as he had not submitted the correct application at the beginning of the war, he was therefore entitled to nothing.[3]

Not all the Vale's heroes were public figures. Most were just ordinary men, doing what they saw as ordinary jobs in a very extraordinary time – people like the Revd Gwilym O. Griffith, pastor at Stanwell Road Baptist chapel in Penarth. Initially, he had been vocal in his condemnation of the war, but suffered a change of heart and spent the last few years of the conflict serving quietly and undramatically as a chaplain with the YMCA in France:

> The rats are keeping me company here – snarling and scurrying like dogs, and now and again getting into violent disputes amongst themselves. Outside, the guns are booming – sometimes one long roll like the noise of orchestral drums, sometimes heavy individual thuds, like the banging of iron doors.[4]

Pastor Griffith wrote the above letter to the *Penarth Times* from a YMCA hut behind the lines. He put away the letter when two Welsh boys came in and he sang hymns with them for a few hours. As he later appended to the letter, he would not have wanted to be anywhere else in the world.

Gunner Arthur Eveleigh from Newland Street in Barry served with the Anti-Aircraft Battery of the Royal Garrison Artillery, an unromantic and unacknowledged job if ever there was one. However, even anti-aircraft gunners deserved a little fame and in 1917 Eveleigh wrote home to his parents about a success he and his battery had just enjoyed, bringing down L32, a German airship engaged in a raid on London: 'It was a lovely sight to see the Zeppelin burning in the air and I just wish you could have seen it.'[5]

Bringing down a Zeppelin was a major victory and, for a while at least, Gunner Eveleigh revelled in his fifteen minutes of fame. He even sent a piece of the fabric from the airship to his old school, Gladstone Road.

Penarth's first Victoria Cross winner was Richard William Leslie Wain. Although he was born in Victoria Square, Penarth, he actually had firmer links with the nearby village of Sully and with Llandaff where his father was a solicitor. As a young man Wain was always interested in engineering, and after gaining his commission in July 1915 he eventually transferred to the new Tank Corps.

On 20 November 1917 during the Battle of Cambrai, when tanks were first used in an effective way, Richard Wain was commander of A Battalion. When he noticed a German strong point holding up the British advance, he directed his tank to the spot, but when he was within feet of the target his tank was hit by a shell. Wain and one other were the only survivors.

Despite terrible injuries, Wain managed to crawl out, find a machine gun and attack the German strong point. When his ammunition was used, he picked up a discarded rifle and continued to fire at the retreating Germans until he was finally shot in the head and killed. His Victoria Cross was awarded posthumously.

Some Vale heroes achieved distinction after the war had ended. Emily Ada Pickford, married to one of the owners of the *Penarth Times*, was a renowned singer who gave hundreds of concerts for wounded soldiers during the war years. After November 1918, with thousands of surplus soldiers simply 'kicking their heels' waiting for discharge, she was asked to organise and run a concert party to entertain the troops.

After a concert at Guoy in France, two cars were provided to transport the party to their next venue. The road was icy and Emily's car skidded off the towpath into the River Somme. Several of the performers were rescued from the freezing water but Emily was never seen again. She is the only woman listed on the First World War section of the Penarth war memorial.

Penarth's most distinguished war hero was undoubtedly Sam Pearce. Born in Arcot Street in the town, he and his family were all popular members of the Salvation Army Band, in which the young Sam was an accomplished performer on the French horn. The family moved to Australia in 1911 but, with the coming of war, Sam and his brothers returned to join the Army.

Sam Pearce saw service in the Gallipoli campaign and was later awarded the Military Medal for bravery during a skirmish on the Menin Road. When peace was declared, Sam was at home, convalescing with a foot wound. Four years of war had given him a love of adventure, however, and in 1919, rather than settle down to a peaceful existence, he signed on to fight against the Bolsheviks as part of the North Russia Expeditionary Force.

Sam Pearce arrived in Archangel on 11 July 1919 and, along with the rest of his comrades, was soon marching through the frozen landscape to Emptsa, where his unit was ordered to attack a series of strong concrete blockhouses. Pinned down by accurate enemy fire, Sam Pearce rushed the buildings, cut through the coils of barbed wire and threw several Mills bombs into the strongholds. As he moved away, he was hit by machine-gun fire. Unfortunately the Bolsheviks had been using dum-dum bullets and, with an artery severed, Sam Pearce slowly bled to death. He was awarded a posthumous VC.[6]

The rugby international Captain John L. Williams was one of the leading lights in the Cardiff City (Pals) Battalion that was decimated during the battle for Mametz Wood. Williams was one of the casualties: 'We regret to state that Mrs Williams has received official intimation of the death from wounds of her husband Captain JL Williams, the famous Cardiff and Wales International football player.'[7]

Soon after the battle had ended, Mrs Williams had received a postcard from her husband, stating that he was not seriously wounded. It was followed by a letter saying that he had been struck by shrapnel and that his leg had been amputated. Then came the sudden and totally unexpected news of his death.

John Angel Gibbs was one of the directors of the Gibbs Shipping Company of Cardiff. Married to Gladys Morel, of the Morel shipping family, John Gibbs was thirty-four years old when war broke out and had little need to join up. Nevertheless, he promptly enlisted in the Glamorgan Yeomanry and was later commissioned into the Welsh Regiment.

Somewhat older than the other officers, John Gibbs was given the nickname Uncle – a name later used by R. C. Sherriff in his play *Journey's End*. Gibbs was a good soldier, being Mentioned in Dispatches and then awarded the DSO. He achieved quick promotion and was soon second in command of the 9th Battalion.

The writer Ford Madox Heuffer served briefly with the battalion, and thought highly of 'Uncle' Gibbs. He included him, under his real name, in the third volume of his sequence *Parade's End*. The book is a work of fiction, but the portrayal of Gibbs seems to be both accurate and realistic. Heuffer was no soldier and did not stay long with the battalion, but John Gibbs, now Major, was named as forward commander of the battalion for the Battle of the Menin Road.

It was 20 September 1917 and in the early dawn, an hour before going 'over the top', John Gibbs wrote to his wife, 'This will be the proudest moment of my life, as I know my Battalion will live up to its reputation.'

Major John Angel Gibbs was shot and carried to a dressing station in the early stages of the battle. He died of his wounds later in the day.[8]

Above: Sam Pearce from Penarth won his VC in 1919, fighting for the White Russians against the Bolsheviks. He is shown here as a young boy, sitting third from the right, in a photograph of the Penarth Salvation Army Band.

Below left: John Angel Gibbs, of the Gibbs Shipping Company in Cardiff, leaves Buckingham Palace after receiving the DSO in 1916, accompanied by his wife. Gibbs was killed the following year on the Menin Road.

Below right: John Gibbs, standing at the rear, is shown here with fellow officers. One of them (right) is the writer Ford Madox Heuffer who included Gibbs in his book *No More Parades*, keeping his real name and his nickname, Uncle.

Frank Gaskell, a man with Cardiff and Llantwit Major connections, served with the 2nd Battalion of the Welsh Regiment in the early days of the war. However, he was wounded in the jaw and invalided home. While he was recovering from these injuries at home in Llanishen he was asked to become involved with the formation of the Cardiff City Battalion. He duly became their commanding officer with the rank of lieutenant colonel.

Gaskell was injured again in December 1915 when a fall from his horse caused a fracture of his leg. He again recuperated at home in Llanishen but was back with the battalion by April 1916. The following month he was killed by a sniper while inspecting battalion lines at Merville. Some accounts say that the sniper's bullet hit the colonel's ammunition pouch and his death was caused by the exploding rounds.

Two Welsh airmen, Dan Evans from Barry and Thomas Rees from Cardiff, have the dubious distinction of being victims of the German ace Baron Manfred von Richthofen, the Red Baron.

Dan Evans had been working in the West Indies when war broke out, but returned to enlist in the Royal Welsh Fusiliers. After gaining a commission he transferred to the Royal Flying Corps, flying antiquated BE2C machines in reconnaissance missions over enemy lines. On 29 April 1917, at the end of what was known as 'Bloody April' because so many British aircraft were shot down, he encountered von Richthofen and did not return. His body was never recovered.

Thomas Rees was the observer in an outdated FE2B machine when, on 17 September 1916, his formation fell in with a group of new Albatross fighters led by the ace Oswald Boelcke and including an eager new flyer, Manfred von Richthofen. Rees managed to keep the enemy away for some time but, eventually, von Richthofen got in a burst of fire that crippled the FE's engine and mortally wounded both pilot and observer. It was von Richthofen's first recorded victory.[9]

Arguably, the greatest heroes from Cardiff, Penarth, Barry and the Vale were the countless, unheralded – and often unacknowledged – sailors of the Merchant Navy fleet. Without their grim determination and selfless courage the war could never have been won. Unarmed and facing a hidden enemy who gave them little or no chance of survival, they ploughed on regardless and, ultimately, did as much to ensure victory as any of the fighting men. Theirs was an unglamorous war but it was one that had to be fought and won.

*

If the Vale produced men of exceptional courage and bravery, it also managed to come up with quite a few villains as well.

On 10 November the *South Wales Echo* proudly announced that Cardiff soldier Sergeant Major White was recuperating at the home of his father-in-law in the city. White, of the Army Service Corps, said the paper, was about to receive the Victoria Cross for bravery during the recent battles at Mons and Le Cateau. He had been escorting a supply convoy when they were ambushed by a party of German Uhlans. Despite being outnumbered, White had attacked, wielding his sword, and put the enemy cavalry to flight.

As if this wasn't enough, Sgt Major White realised that his officer, Captain Grey, had been wounded and left on the field of the skirmish. White went back to the spot and, despite being shot in both legs, promptly rescued the officer.[10]

Just four days later, the paper was forced to reveal the sad truth: 'Yesterday Company Sergeant Major Mouser and Farrier Sergeant Spiller arrived in Cardiff from the Curragh with orders to escort White to his regiment. It is a fact that White has not been in France since the outbreak of war.'[11]

As a Reservist, White had apparently re-enlisted at Cardiff in August and had been sent to Aldershot before being transferred to the Curragh. Promoted to CSM he had been given leave to visit Cardiff – and his sick wife: 'He is of abstemious habit and it is presumed that his story was due to hallucinations, as a result of recurring malaria.'[12]

The behaviour of soldiers, particularly when off duty, was a perpetual cause of concern. In early September 1914 the public houses of Penarth were all served with early-closing notices in an attempt to decrease the amount of drunkenness caused by soldiers. According to the local paper, the measure was hugely successful but it brought a furious response from Captain A. P. Thomas, officer in charge of the Royal Garrison Artillery at Penarth Fort. In a controlled but angry response to the paper, Thomas listed his objections and rebuttals: 'Firstly, no men from this Battery are ever out after 7.30 p.m. And secondly, sixty percent of the men are total abstainers.'[13]

It seems an amazing claim to make for a group of red-blooded soldiery but Captain Thomas was proud of his men, and his rebuttal of the accusations was accepted without argument.

Other complaints about soldiers were altogether more substantial. In October 1914 three women in Barry were attacked by a man in Army uniform who pushed them to the ground and then assaulted them. The man was Patrick John Callaghan, a Territorial who had recently been posted to the town. He was arrested and sentenced to a one-month imprisonment. Colonel East, Commander in Chief of the Severn Defences, then issued an order banning all women from the pubs in the town – a clear case of locking the door after the horse had bolted.

Although originally from London, William Edward Herbert had been working at Barry Docks as a marine donkeyman when war broke out. He enlisted and achieved rapid promotion, although he was soon reduced to the rank of corporal after several instances of drunkenness. On 10 July 1916 he was placed on a charge for refusing an order from Sergeant Whitfield and Corporal Fox. His defence was that he was being victimised by two young and inexperienced NCOs.

At 4.30 a.m. the following morning, Herbert went into the hut at the Transport Lines where Whitfield and Fox were sleeping and shot them both dead as they lay in their bunks. He then went outside and, using a piece of wood he had previously carved, put his rifle to his mouth, pushed the wood onto the trigger and blew his brains out.[14]

Herbert's action was both serious and fatal but there were many other minor instances of bad behaviour among sailors and the troops. In 1918 John Kendrick and John Brennan of the SS *Balmore* were charged with stealing the ship's compass as she lay at Barry – the compass being valued at £15. They were sentenced to two months' hard labour.

Other offences earned lighter sentences. When, in May 1916, seaman Joseph Jenkins appeared before Cardiff Police Court for failing to join a transport, his defence was that he did not join the ship because he had wanted a Christmas holiday. The bench took a lenient view as this was his first offence and he had already served on three previous transports. On being 'let off', the defendant vowed it would never happen again.[15]

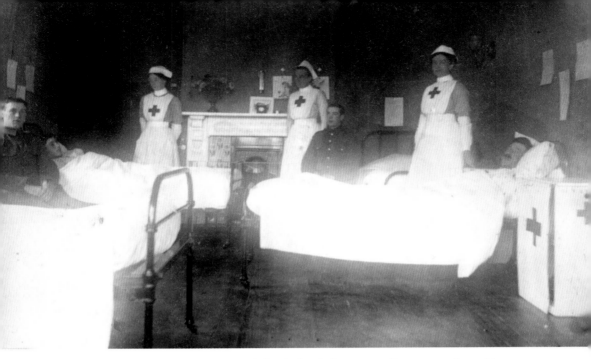

One of the many hospital wards set up in Cardiff to deal with the never-ending stream of casualties.

In January 1915 Rifleman William Woods was charged with disorderly conduct after a fracas in Bute Street and in the Golden Cross pub in Cardiff. He also assaulted the policeman who tried to arrest him. Serving with the Munster Rifles and being home in Cardiff on leave, Woods commented, 'I have been drunk since I have been on furlough.' He was fined twenty shillings or, failing to pay, a jail sentence of twenty-one days.[16]

Civilians were not exempt from dubious behaviour, either. In May 1916 Dr Samuel Wallace was summoned under the new lighting order which forbade the showing of bright lights after dark, an early system of blackout that was enormously unpopular. Many people thought the Home Office Order quite stupid as, although the lights of the city were obviously bright, there was little chance of any airship arriving over Cardiff, Penarth or Barry.

Whether or not Dr Wallace was one of the doubters will never be known. However, on 22 April his house, on the corner of Marlborough Road and Pen y Lan Road, was apparently lit up like a Christmas tree, none of the windows being screened or curtained in any way.

Dr Wallace could not be in court but was represented by his solicitor who said that Dr Wallace's son had left the lights on. Evidence was presented that Dr Wallace had shouted at the policeman who knocked on his door and said he could 'go to the Devil!' If he had his boots on, he shouted, he would come out and kick the policeman down the steps. The solicitor apologised profusely, and Dr Wallace was cautioned and ordered to pay costs.[17]

In a time of intense patriotism, those who refused to fight were regarded as villains of the worst sort. There was little or no recognition of the fact that to take a stance as a conscientious objector was, in its way, as brave as charging across No Man's Land into a hail of enemy fire. The punishments handed out were draconian, to say the least: 'Sentences on nine conscientious objectors who were tried by Court Martial at Cardiff Barracks last week for insubordination were promulgated on parade this morning in the presence of 300 men who had returned from the front.'[18]

All of the men were sentenced to 112 days' hard labour and sent to Cardiff jail. The convicted COs included Morgan Jones, a well-known district councillor from Bargoed, and schoolteacher Herbert Davies. It is not hard to imagine the response the conscientious objectors got from seasoned fighting men just back from France.

For real villains, you have to look no further than the men of Cardiff City Corporation who 'downed tools' on 6 May 1918, demanding £1 more in their wage packets – and this while the war was still raging on the Western Front. It meant that all rubbish clearance from the city streets immediately stopped. Despite an assurance that their claims would be considered, this was not satisfactory, and on 15 July they struck again – as the papers said, 'a prerogative not shared by their fellow citizens at the front.'[19] This time they were demanding a war bonus of over three shillings a shift, as well as a bonus on overtime.

The dispute ground on for several weeks, and the air in Cardiff was not good as the mounds of refuse and rubbish grew steadily higher. Eventually, drastic action was called for:

Lonely Cardiff pedestrians at midnight, which was inky black, were astonished on turning the Hayes Corner into Queen Street, which was comparatively brilliant through the full glare of a few electric lights, to find the Lord Mayor engaged in scavenging. Aided by a stalwart band of twelve aldermen and councillors, with one boy, there was the pride of civic life wielding a scavengers shovel and revelling in the task of loading a truck with horse manure.[20]

The work began at midnight and was completed by 3.00 a.m. It was not without a degree of interruption, however, as when the mayor and his party reached the Empire Theatre a group of strikers suddenly appeared, shouting abuse, calling the councillors 'civic blacklegs' and threatening to tip over the mayoral rubbish cart. Only when a number of police appeared did the crowd finally disperse.

The strike was eventually settled a few days later when the men agreed to return to work provided their case was put before a conciliation board. The municipal workers of Cardiff were not alone in striking during the war years. Miners, munitions workers, bakers and railwaymen all withdrew their labour at one time or another, an action hardly guaranteed to gain them much favour in the eyes of the men at the front.

8

War on the Home Front

As the war progressed, conditions for those men and women left behind in the Vale changed and, undoubtedly, deteriorated. Yet to begin with there was nothing but enthusiasm for the war, and much public sorrow for its victims, people like Nurse Cavell who was executed by the Germans for helping British soldiers to escape from behind enemy lines: 'On Sunday next at 3.00 p.m. a Memorial Service for Miss Edith Cavell, who was diabolically murdered in Brussels, will be held in St Augustine's Church.'[1]

Not everyone could enlist, of course. Some, like the band of Sea Scouts from Barry who were taken on as signalmen in the coaling fleet that operated in and out of the port, were just too young. For those at the other end of the spectrum, however, there was also work to be done. Both Penarth and Barry raised Volunteer Training Corps or Town Guards, early precursors of the Second World War's Home Guard.

The Barry Town Guard was formed and began operations as early as September 1914, the men being drilled by a police sergeant who had once served in the Grenadier Guards. By the end of the month, over 400 men had joined.[2]

As more and more men went into the Army, their positions as munitions workers, clerks, typists or bus conductors were taken over by women, much to the disgust of the more reactionary citizens. It was a time of revolutionary change, both socially and economically. Dozens of women left domestic service for better-paid but more dangerous jobs in the munitions industry. Women were beginning to flex their muscles and, for the men of the Vale, it was not always a comfortable situation:

> On Sunday evening a young woman passed down Glebe Street and through Windsor Road complacently and brazenly smoking a cigar with all the ease and frankness of a veteran of the weed. In Windsor Road a number of boys looked like making a demonstration and following the woman but she was allowed to proceed unmolested.[3]

The sensibilities of Penarth residents were clearly shocked – it was something they were going to have to get used to in the years ahead.

There was, of course, a downside. By 1916 many women, deprived of husbands and fathers and clearly seeking a little solace, were resorting to alcohol. In a retrospective article, published some fifty years later, one Cardiff newspaper commented on the large numbers of drunken

An advertisement for the Penarth Volunteer Training Corps, forerunner of the Home Guard. Look at the line at the bottom of the advert – 'No Shirkers Need Apply.'

women on the city streets: 'Deaths by alcohol, it was alleged, had increased by 104 per cent, apart from the nauseating and degrading spectacle of women glorying in their inebriety as they sang music hall ditties in the streets.'[4]

The paper went on to quote a minister of religion who set out to investigate the phenomenon. He watched one public house for just thirty-five minutes and in that time he managed to count 115 women coming out of the pub, laden down with flagons and jugs of beer.

The increasing drunkenness – of men as well as women – was one of the reasons for David Lloyd George introducing licensing hours in May 1916, pubs closing two and a half hours earlier each evening. In Lloyd George's inimitable words, 'We are fighting Germans, Austrians and Drink, and so far as I can see the greatest of these deadly foes is Drink.'[5]

Lloyd George's stringencies seemed to work. By the middle part of 1918 the consumption of alcohol had been reduced by almost half.

*

Plans had been laid, before the war, to provide hospital accommodation for wounded troops, particularly in the city of Cardiff, but the sheer number of casualties that were soon pouring into the country took everyone by surprise. Cardiff Infirmary was at the centre of the provision, 100 beds having been made available to the Army. It was never going to be enough.

Several Cardiff schools, places like Albany Road, Ninian Park and Lansdowne, were quickly transformed into hospitals, the pupils having to share facilities and working just half days in school – much to their enjoyment. During the first few days of the Battle of the Somme these schools received well over 300 casualties. As the *South Wales Echo* reported on 4 July 1916, four days after the battle began,

Wounded soldiers to the number of 320 from the Front arrived at Cardiff at 4-o-clock this afternoon. All the cases were sitting cases, the injuries being mostly gunshot wounds, and the majority were able to walk unaided to the motors which were waiting. Some of the Tommies, who appeared in capital spirits, were wounded as recently as yesterday morning. The soldiers were distributed to Howardian (40), King Edward VII Hospital (10), Albany Road (70), Splott (50), Lansdowne (75), Ninian Park (75).[6]

It was not long before Cardiff and all of the Vale were inundated with wounded soldiers. This photograph shows walking wounded detraining at Whitchurch in the north of the city.

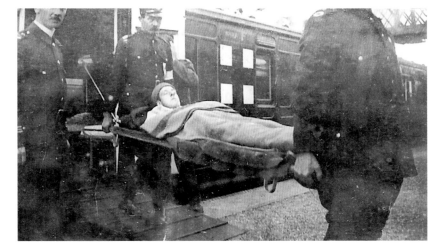

More serious casualties were transported on stretchers and taken to one of the many Cardiff hospitals.

Schools in Cardiff and Barry were often converted into temporary hospitals, but the cottage hospitals of smaller communities were also used for wounded soldiers.

It is no wonder that the soldiers were happy. They were out of the carnage of battle, for a few months at least! Another Red Cross train arrived in Cardiff at the end of July, containing a further 213 wounded soldiers, about 100 of them being reported as 'Anzacs'. Once again, the comment was made that the men seemed happy to be in Cardiff. They were again distributed to the various local hospitals.

Soldiers were dealt with effectively and efficiently, wherever they were sent to recover and recuperate. As far as the military authorities were concerned, the primary purpose of the hospitals was to treat the men and get them back to the front as quickly as possible:

> Today there are 2000 beds … In Cardiff alone there are beds for 1100 patients in the sectional hospitals of the 3rd Western General Hospital. Almost 10,000 patients from overseas have passed in and out of the Cardiff hospitals for treatment, and the death rate has been only three to the thousand.[7]

The longer the war went on, the greater the need for hospital beds became, and wounded soldiers in their distinctive blue dungarees were a common sight around the city. As late as February 1918 the Prince of Wales visited Cardiff in order to open the former Mansion House as a hospital for soldiers who had lost limbs in the war.

In 1915 Whitchurch Hospital, the mental amenity for the city and surrounding areas, was taken over as a general medical and surgical war hospital. The majority of the mental patients were transferred to places like Carmarthen and Talgarth, although forty-five male patients were retained in order to work on the hospital farm.

The medical superintendent, Dr Edwin Goodall, was commissioned into the Army Medical Corps, and the existing staff were retained to run the hospital on military lines. Whitchurch took its first convoy of wounded soldiers on 16 June 1915 and by the end of the war over 12,000 troops had been treated at the hospital. A few of the more emotionally damaged men remained at Whitchurch once the war ended and the hospital returned to its normal duties.

Small cottage hospitals across the Vale of Glamorgan also took patients during the war. Barry, with its population of about 36,000, provided no fewer than 437 hospital beds during the conflict and was the site of the first VAD hospital in Wales.[8]

The infamous Spanish flu epidemic that ravaged the country in 1918 reached Barry that November, when ten deaths were recorded. There were other deaths, usually from pneumonia, which inevitably followed in the wake of flu. Schools were closed and the hospital beds were full, although most people were treated at home.

In Cardiff the flu epidemic accounted for dozens more, 125 people dying in just one week in October. Shops and offices closed because there were simply not enough healthy people to keep them open, and, yet again, schools were shut. There were not enough carpenters available to make the necessary coffins.[9] It seemed such an unjust reward after years of hardship and pain.

*

As the war ground on and the German U-boat campaign began to intensify, serious food shortages began to affect not just the Vale of Glamorgan but all of the country. Before the war Britain had imported almost 60 per cent of its food, and it was clear to the German High Command that the surest way to defeat Britain lay not in face-to-face combat but in depriving her people of essential foodstuffs.

Losses to surface raiders and U-boats gradually increased, every ship that went to the bottom taking with it valuable supplies of grain, wheat, sugar and corn. By the autumn of 1916, farmers in the Vale of Glamorgan were having to produce more food with fewer farmhands and considerably fewer horses – by the end of the war over 1 million horses had been requisitioned by the Army for use in the battle zones. By and large, the farmers' problems went unrecognised by the general public, as people were convinced that farmers were keeping the best for themselves.

Prices rose sharply during the war years – another reason people thought farmers were little more than profiteers. However, price rises were not just for food. The price of beer rose steadily, Cardiff Licensed Victuallers increasing the price of a pint to four pence (three and a half pence for outdoor sales) as early as May 1916.[10]

Lord Devonport, the food controller, was clear that everyone needed to cut back on what they ate, yet the government was loath to impose food rationing, as such an imposition would be a terrible blow to morale – after all, acknowledging that Britain was effectively under siege would be an acknowledgement that the Royal Navy no longer 'ruled the waves'.

By the spring of 1917, school attendance in Cardiff was being badly affected as parents detailed their children to stand in food queues rather than turn up for education. That March the city council, only too aware of the problem, announced that no potatoes would be served

Above left: As the German submarine blockade intensified, food shortages became a serious problem, and queues were soon a part of everyday life.

Above right: Items that most people had previously taken for granted – things like potatoes, bread and margarine – became highly prized possessions as the food shortage grew worse. At least the comic artists could laugh at the predicament, as this postcard shows.

to children during school hours. Bakers were forbidden to make fancy cakes, and restaurants were allowed only two ounces of flour for each meal they served.[11]

Voluntary food rationing was introduced first but it met with only limited success. Food queues continued to lengthen and, by January 1918, 'people were now flocking from one shop to another. Many failed to follow the queues and being thus unable to obtain food, the children had to suffer.'[12]

Finally, in April 1918, compulsory food rationing was introduced. People had been encouraged to grow their own vegetables for many months. Lawns were dug up, flower beds turned over to vegetable growing, while open land in places like Roath Park and Llandaff Fields in the city had been ploughed over for allotments in the spring of 1917. Even the grounds of Cardiff Castle were turned over to agricultural use. Nevertheless, there was still a terrible shortage of available land, and during 1917, out of 1,000 applications for allotments in the city barely 300 had been supplied.

Of course, there were some commodities that you just could not grow – even if you had an allotment or a big enough garden in the first place. Butter and margarine were in short supply throughout the war, but by 1918 they were virtually unattainable, as one anonymous poet wrote in the *Penarth Times*:

> Oh margarine, oh margarine,
> Thy absence causes many a scene.
> I stand in queues mid snow and rain
> To get some more of Thee again.
> Fed up with jam and bloater paste,
> Oh margo, come to me in haste![13]

The ability to laugh at such predicaments was not a uniquely British talent, but when it came to food shortages the people of the Vale were in a league of their own:

> Oh where, and oh where, can our taters be?
> We've none for dinner, and no sugar for tea.
> The farmer has plenty, we know full well,
> But the shops are empty, there's no taters to sell.[14]

The farms of the Vale were hit by wart disease early in 1918, with crops in and around Barry, Wenvoe, Cadoxton, Cowbridge and Bridgend being particularly badly affected. Shortages were one thing, disease like this was something else. Economically, it placed a huge strain on the Vale and on the country as a whole: 'The loss to this country owing to wart disease is very considerable, surely not less in current coin than £35,000.'[15]

*

Children, of course, took it all in their stride. There were far more important things to do, things like playing games. For children in rural areas like St Athan, such games were usually quite homespun, as Harry Griffith Jenkins remembered:

We used to cut nut sticks. We'd most of us been given the heads of old golf clubs and we just fitted these onto the nut sticks. We'd find lost balls on the old Lays Golf Course – it's gone now, under the power station but a lovely course, it was. We used to go up the fields. There was a little river running across and the great thing was to hit your ball over this. We made tees out of mounds of earth.

We used to cut holes out of the ground and sometimes we'd play for half pence a hole. I was always there, playing. If I broke my stick, I'd cut another one and go home. Then I'd have to burn out the remains of the broken nut stick and fit the new one in.

I suppose it must have helped me because, later on, I joined the artisans section of the Lays. By the time I was eighteen I was a single figure handicapper.[16]

For children from the towns and cities, playing games was still the most important element in their lives, no matter what might be happening on the war front. Ernest Plumb was born in Caerleon in 1910 but moved to Cardiff after his father died:

We seemed to spend our lives just playing, usually in the street. We'd play tops, spinning tops, and hop scotch – boys and girls played that. And we had iron hoops. We'd bowl these along the road, hitting them with a stick to keep them rolling.

We used to collect cigarette cards. You'd get them in packs of Gold Flake and other brands. You'd collect them in sets. And you played a game with them, out in the street. You'd flick a card out onto the pavement and the other boys had to cover it. If they did, your card became theirs.[17]

For girls like Megan Rees, skipping was the game that mattered. She and her friends would use the orange string off orange boxes for their rope:

Sometimes the rope would stretch right across the street with a girl on each end, turning the rope. And all the girls would be skipping. There was no traffic to bother you in those days.

Before the lamp lighter came around with his big pole, you would tie the rope to the top of the lamp post. And then you'd swing round and round. That was really great fun. Then we'd play games like catty and dog. You had two bits of stick, one long, one little. Your father would sharpen one end of the small stick with his pen knife. You'd tap the small stick with the big one and see how long you could get it to spin.[18]

The one thing that almost every child remembered about the war was fear of Zeppelins. The fear was perhaps greater than the reality and when, on rare occasions, a balloon was spotted – probably a British airship rather than an enemy Zeppelin – it was the novelty of the sighting that struck home, as Alice Josephine Richards remembered: 'We saw one of the early Zeppelins go over. We got out of our bedroom window and sat on the kitchen roof to watch her go over. I remember all the lights, underneath she was all lit up, you know, where the people were. It was a wonderful sight.'[19]

Harry Griffith Jenkins recalled,

We saw a balloon once. Mum had gone shopping and she came racing back. She thought it was a Zeppelin – it probably wasn't. But it was big enough, believe me.

Mum was exhausted, she'd been running all the way from St Athan. 'Get in the house', she was crying, 'get in the house'. What good she thought that would do I don't know. If it was a Zeppelin and it dropped a bomb it would have blown up half the village, never mind our house.[20]

9

The End of the War

The year 1918 brought food rationing but it also brought the Americans. The USA had finally joined the war in 1917 – as an independent sovereign power rather than an ally, but it took time to mobilise her troops and it was 1918 before the 'doughboys' began arriving in great numbers. Barry was one of the most popular points of disembarkation for the arriving Americans, being both safe and relatively close to the Atlantic sea lanes.

The arrival of the Americans created quite a stir in war-weary Barry, where people could remember the parades of the early war years when enthusiasm and expectations had been high. So to see these fresh-faced, fit and well-fed American soldiers was something of a thrill. They were welcomed by the sounding of ship's sirens and train whistles while some of the vessels in the docks even flew bunting. For the children of the town it was an occasion that was almost too good to be true:

> One day during the summer of 1918 we heard that some new troops had arrived at the docks and that they were going to march up through the main shopping centre at Holton Road. … Why were these troops so special? When I reached Holton Road all the soldiers were lined up outside the Town Hall and King's Square. What a sight they were. Great tall men in tight uniforms and boy scout hats! The Yanks had finally arrived.[1]

In Cardiff the welcome was equally ecstatic. The weather was beautiful, perfect for the occasion – it really did seem as if it was a new dawn after four years of unmitigated grind and horror. The Yanks had arrived, now everything would be all right: 'Today Cardiff, in common with Newport and Barry, is doing honour to the American troops. Cardiff's reception was whole hearted. The citizens turned out in great force, and this despite the fact that, owing to unavoidable delay in the troops arrival, people had to wait several hours.'[2]

The arrival of the Americans was one moment of joy in what was an otherwise gloomy year. In May the situation regarding shortages reached even the weekly and daily newspapers, with the Government Department for the Control of Paper Supply ordering that they should either reduce the size of their issues or increase the price. Papers such as the *Barry Dock News* chose, initially, to increase the price, but within the month they had been forced to reduce the size by a third as well.

The Yanks are here! American troops began arriving in great numbers in the early part of 1918, and Barry was one of the ports where they disembarked – much to the delight of the local schoolchildren.

Work in the three Vale of Glamorgan docks continued apace as the Allied armies in France began to prepare for what would eventually be the last big push of the war. Inevitably, there were accidents.

On Thursday 11 July a crane at Windsor Slipway in Cardiff Docks toppled into the water while removing an anchor from a ship moored at the jetty. The crane's shoring arms were not in use, and the footbrake, which should have released the load, was not used. The crane driver, Mr William Jenkins, was killed in the accident.

In Penarth that summer there was an outbreak of petty crime. At the end of August a Russian ship in the docks was burgled, thieves managing to get away with a rich haul of money, watches and other valuables from the crew's quarters. Considering the high level of security on the dock gates, it had to be an 'inside job', but the police were never able to get to the bottom of the affair and the culprits escaped without punishment.[3]

By the autumn of 1918 the Allies had gained the upper hand in France and, inevitably, people's minds began to turn to the ways they could commemorate their dead. It was not something that could be taken lightly.

There had never been such a catastrophic loss of life in any previous war. In Britain alone, 614,000 servicemen, 145,000 merchant seamen and 1,117 civilians had died, thousands more being grievously wounded and maimed. It was as if a whole generation had been snatched away.[4]

Previously, memorials to ordinary soldiers and sailors had been rare. The men of the Napoleonic and Crimean Wars, even the more recent Boer War, did not warrant commemoration in the eyes of the public. They were professional soldiers who must expect death as an occupational hazard.

The Roll of Honour in St Augustine's church, Penarth.

However, this war of 1914–18 was a volunteers' war, and the families and friends of the dead demanded recognition. Beginning with people's shrines – simple flowers or crosses at the roadside or on street corners – the way was clear. Each town or village that had lost men in the war would commemorate them with a war memorial.

A letter from a man called William Dooley in the *Barry Dock News* in October 1916 showed the way things should go. Besides offering to help start a subscription list for the town, Dooley was clear that the Barry dead must be remembered: 'There are few streets or parts of Barry that have not had the cruel side of war brought vividly home … already other towns have had their memorials unveiled.'[5]

Mr Dooley may have been stretching the truth a little. War memorials had not been unveiled, although several towns, like Penarth, kept a Roll of Honour in a local church or chapel. The people of Penarth had theirs in St Augustine's church, while in September 1918 a calvary was also erected at nearby All Saints church as a temporary memorial to the twenty-three members of the congregation who had died. The time for formal war memorials would come later.

*

When peace came at last at 11.00 a.m. on 11 November 1918, it was at first greeted with a degree of subdued relief in the towns and villages of the Vale. That relief soon gave way to wild excitement.

In Cardiff, peace was announced by the sounding of the siren of the *Western Mail* blasting out, loud and compelling above the daily hubbub of city traffic. It was soon joined by hooters and sirens from ships in the docks, and crowds began to gather in the streets. Schools were hurriedly closed for the day and two American officers who happened to be walking down St Mary's Street were mobbed and wrapped up in a gigantic Union Jack by a group of overenthusiastic shop assistants.[6]

In front of City Hall, the Lord Mayor read out a formal message from Lloyd George, stating that the war had ended. Crowds celebrated for the rest of the day, and that evening thanksgiving services were held in churches across the city.

It was the same in the rest of the Vale. Crowds gathered in every street or town square, content to just stand or sing the National Anthem. Even the villages joined in the celebrations. Harry Griffith Jenkins of St Athan recalled,

> I don't remember too much about the village celebrations when peace finally came. I think I was more interested in seeing relatives come home and the way we celebrated that. That meant more to me, I think.
>
> But I do remember a big bonfire and lots of torches in the darkness. More than anything I remember the flags. They must have been flying out of everyone's windows. Goodness only knows where mum and the rest got them. The only time I'd seen so many flags was when I was in Barry with mum and a regiment of soldiers came marching past, from Buttrills Camp. They were off to France and everyone was waving a flag of some sort.[7]

Flag making – from all sorts of leftover material – was second nature to most people in those days. Occasionally, purpose-made flags were bought despite the expense. Waving them was

Armistice Day, 11 November 1918, was a day of huge national celebration. Once again, the comic artists took the events in their stride.

something that children did quite happily – even if, sometimes, like Augusta Clubb, they got things slightly wrong:

> On Armistice Day I was ill in bed. You were usually confined to bed when you weren't well in those days. Anyway, I heard a lorry coming down the road. It was full of airmen and they were going into town to celebrate. I grabbed a flag. We always had lots of them in the house, my mother was the commander of the local VADs in town so we always had them, just in case they were needed. I ran to the window and opened it, then stuck my head out and started to wave the flag.
>
> The men in the lorry all waved back, cheering and laughing. And then I realised I'd been waving a Russian flag. I told my mother but she just laughed. 'I don't suppose they minded,' she said.
>
> There was great cheering and excitement everywhere that day, all over town. Everybody was so happy. Then a year later, in the summer of 1919, we had the Victory Parade. My mother was marching with the VADs. I was so proud of her. I remember she had a walking stick with a silver knob head. All through the town they went. It was such a lovely sunny day.[8]

In Barry, at 11 o'clock sharp, all the ships in the docks sounded their whistles. The call was taken up by the workshops on the dockside, and men came streaming from their places of employment. Teachers quickly realised that it would be impossible to keep children at their desks, and all the schools in the town promptly closed for the day.

The whole week was then devoted to peace celebrations. These culminated in a huge torchlight procession on Friday 15 November. There were bands, people in fancy dress, soldiers and Boy Scouts – everyone who wanted to get involved took part. It all ended in Kings Square, where an effigy of the Kaiser was set alight and burned: '[The dummy was] set on fire and reduced to ashes amid a scene of great excitement and enthusiasm, the only regret being that the Arch-Demoniac himself was not present to submit to the fiery ordeal.'[9]

*

With the coming of peace it was time to think seriously about war memorials for the fallen. Herbert Thompson had first suggested a Welsh National War Memorial back in 1917 and two years later, in 1919, the *Western Mail* opened a fund to build the monument. In all, over £30,000 was raised and the memorial was erected in Queen Alexandra Gardens. It was dedicated by the Archbishop of Wales on 12 June 1928.

Figures of a soldier, sailor and airman guard the three porches through which entry to the monument and its sunken courtyard can be made. A Book of Remembrance, containing the names of over 30,000 Welshmen who had died in the conflict, was presented to Lord Aberdare. That book is now kept at the Temple of Peace in Cardiff.

Barry had numerous memorials in schools and churches, the main focal point being the new Memorial Hall, complete with a cenotaph in front. Designed by Major E. R. Hinchcliffe and built from Portland stone, the building was not completed until 1932. Building a hall such as this to commemorate the dead was not to the liking of some, many thinking it was wrong to build a place where people could dance on the graves of the dead.

WAR MEMORIAL, CARDIFF.

Above: The Welsh National War Memorial in Queen Alexandra Gardens, Cardiff – a suitably sombre and impressive monument.

Right: Penarth war memorial, unveiled and dedicated on Remembrance Day 1924.

Penarth war memorial was formally unveiled on 11 November 1924. Designed by William Goscombe John, it depicts a winged victory figure standing on the prow of a ship. The mood of the unveiling ceremony and dedication was sombre and reflective: 'In pouring rain, as if the Heavens were weeping in memory of the brave men who made the supreme sacrifice, the Penarth War Memorial was unveiled in Alexandra Park on Tuesday by two mothers who had each lost three sons in the war. These were Mrs F Bartlett and Mrs P Fitzgerald.'[10]

In a moving ceremony, most of those present were in tears. As soon as the ceremony ended, the rain stopped and the sun shone again.

Penarth, like Barry, had many memorials apart from the main one in the centre of town. These included a sports pavilion and, most unusual of all, a school/orphanage. The J. A. Gibbs Home was founded in 1918 in memory of Major John Angel Gibbs and was situated in the old Taff Railway Hotel in Paget Place. It was run as a nautical training school until the late 1930s, when it was converted into an approved school. It survives to this day, now running as an EBD school called Headlands.

The smaller towns and villages of the Vale also had their war memorials. Twenty-nine names from the First World War are listed on the Cowbridge memorial, a monument that stands before the town hall in the centre of the community. The town, which had a population of just over 1,000, suffered grievously in the war, and people were determined that the fallen would be remembered.

Dances, collections and donations all brought in the necessary money to pay for the memorial, which was eventually dedicated on 11 May 1921. In addition, Holy Cross church erected a memorial window to commemorate the sacrifice of former pupils from Cowbridge Grammar School.

In the nearby village of Llanblethian there are sixteen names on the memorial in the parish church. Included are three brothers: Frank Dunn who was killed in August 1915, John Robert Dunn (20 August 1915) and Hugh Dunn who died in a bathing accident in the final part of the war.[11]

The St Athan memorial lists just ten names, while nearby Llantwit Major has no fewer than thirty-five. Included on the Llantwit war memorial are Lt-Colonel Frank Gaskell of the Cardiff City Battalion and a VAD nurse, Eva Martha Davies. The memorial was dedicated on 1 October 1921, being positioned on the base of the town's old medieval cross.

Virtually every town, village and city in Britain had suffered casualties in the war. Inevitably the towns and cities, having bigger populations, suffered worst. In some cases the villages were equally badly hit. There were just fifty-two that lost no one – Thankful or Blessed Villages as they are known. Three of them were in Wales. Two of those, Llanfihangel y Creuddyn and Herbrandston, were in west Wales; the third was in the Vale of Glamorgan.

Colwinston sits just 4 miles south of Bridgend, 20 miles west of Cardiff. A tiny and little-visited place, twenty-three men from the village enlisted but all returned unharmed. For a long while it was thought that Colwinston suffered no casualties in the Second World War either, making it one of those rare things, a Doubly Thankful Village.

However, recent research seems to indicate that one man from the village, a relative of the novelist Agatha Christie, died in the Second World War. What is clear is that no casualties were incurred during the First World War, and for that reason alone Colwinston deserved the epithet Thankful Village.

*

The Penarth Hotel of the Taff Vale Railway Company, bought by the widow of Major John Angel Gibbs and given to the National Children's Home and Orphanages (now Action for Children) for use as a nautical training school. It has to be one of the most unusual but most useful of war memorials.

Below left: The memorial at St Athan lists ten men from the village who died in the conflict.

Below right: Llantwit Major war memorial, built on the base of the town's old medieval cross. Listed on the memorial are Lt-Col. Frank Gaskell, commanding officer of the Cardiff City Battalion, and VAD nurse Eva Martha Davies.

The Armistice of November 1918 was not quite the end of Cardiff's involvement in the First World War, even if the following connection was somewhat tenuous.

While a large number of German U-boats were scuttled by their crews as the war was ending, the High Seas Fleet remained intact. After the Battle of Jutland, it had never again ventured out to face the Home Fleet but remained a potent threat to British sea power.

On 21 November 1918, ten days after the Armistice, the High Seas Fleet, consisting of eleven battleships, five battlecruisers and numerous smaller craft, surrendered. The German ships followed in the wake of the light cruiser *Cardiff*, sailing in to the Firth of Forth and, eventually, in to captivity at Scapa Flow.

Cardiff may not have been involved, but a ship bearing the city's name certainly was. The ship's ensign was presented to the Lord Mayor as a memento of an historic occasion.

HMS *Cardiff* leads the German High Seas Fleet into captivity, the last act in a long and bloody campaign.

Conclusion

With the war over, people of the Vale – and the three main towns in particular – could be excused for thinking that things would soon return to normal. It was not to be.

There was, admittedly, an initial boom, particularly as shipowners began to replace lost vessels, and skilled men began to return to the mining and steel industries. Cardiff was soon able to boast that it had 122 shipping companies, making it the largest port in the world. However, world trade quickly collapsed in the aftermath of the war, and by the early 1930s over 60 per cent of the Cardiff ships were laid up.

Coal, previously the staple diet of the three Vale ports, was suddenly in plentiful supply, as the mining and industrial regions of Germany, areas such as the Saar and the Ruhr, had been occupied by Allied forces. This made the acquisition and transportation of the precious fuel far easier for countries such as France, and trade from the Welsh ports began to dry up.

Never again would the three ports reach the incredible export figures of 1913. The pre-war boom years had long gone and, as far as industry was concerned, the future looked bleak – if people cared to look forward at all.

The First World War was a catalyst that changed everything, from the way people lived to the way they viewed their social superiors. Men who had served in the hell of the trenches, as well as women who had achieved a degree of independence and freedom that had been unthought of in 1914, were not going to return, meekly and limply, to the status quo.

It took time, but the old ways, the touching of forelocks and the automatic deference to those in the 'big house' up the lane were gone forever. There was a new social order coming in, and the men, women and children of the Vale would play their parts in making sure the change would be permanent.

Yet it was far from easy. The Depression years were hard and uncompromising, and Cardiff, Penarth and Barry suffered along with everyone else. It was hardly what men had fought for, and it really took the advent of another war to change the fortunes of the country.

In the meantime, however, the boys were back. The war was over and there was every reason to celebrate. For the moment, at least, the future could take care of itself.

Notes

1 The Background

1. John Richards, *Cardiff, A Maritime History*, p. 29.
2. *Ibid.*, p. 30.
3. Phil Carradice, *Penarth: The Story*, p. 5.
4. *Ibid.*, p. 10.
5. Iorwerth Prothero in *Barry: The Centenary Book*, p. 212.
6. Geoffrey North, *Barry*, p. 69.
7. Neil Walklate, *A Step Back: St Nicholas*, p. 57.
8. Phil Carradice, BBC Wales History Blog.
9. Tony Williams in *Southerndown Golf Club*, p. 85.
10. Jose Rawlins, *The Great War: Memorials in Cowbridge and Llanblethian*, p. 10.
11. *South Wales Echo*, 25 July 1914.
12. *Ibid.*

2 And so to War

1. *South Wales Echo*, 15 July 1914.
2. *South Wales Echo*, 3 August 1914.
3. *Ibid.*
4. Interview with Ronnie Phillips, August 1969.
5. *South Wales Echo*, 7 August 1914.
6. Jose Rawlins, pp. 10–11.
7. Phil Carradice, *The Great War: An Illustrated History*, p. 17.
8. *South Wales Echo*, 6 August 1914.
9. *Western Mail*, 4 August 1914.
10. *Penarth Times*, 27 August 1914.
11. *Ibid.*
12. *Penarth Times*, 6 August 1914.

13. *Ibid.*
14. *Penarth Times*, 27 August 1914.
15. Phil Carradice, *A Town in Conflict*, pp. 33–4.
16. *Penarth Times*, 27 August 1914.
17. *Penarth Advertiser*, 25 August 1914.
18. *Ibid.*
19. Trooper S. Townhill, quoted in *A Town in Conflict*, p. 36.
20. Private Frank Pope, quoted in *A Town in Conflict*, p. 36.
21. Anon, quoted in *A Town in Conflict*, p. 36.
22. Private C. A. Cooksey, quoted in *A Town in Conflict*, p. 36.
23. Quoted in Jonathan Hicks, *Barry and the Great War*, p. 5.
24. *Ibid.*, p. 5
25. *South Wales Echo*, 10 August 1914.
26. Phil Carradice, *The Great War*, p. 22.
27. Quoted in Jonathan Hicks, p. 19.
28. *Ibid.*, pp. 11–12.
29. *South Wales Echo*, 7 November 1914.
30. Iorwerth Prothero in *Barry: The Centenary Book*, p. 247.
31. Quoted in Jonathan Hicks, *Barry and the Great War*, p. 8.
32. Peter Stead in *Barry: The Centenary Book*, p. 369.
33. Quoted in Jonathan Hicks, p. 164.
34. Neil Walklate, p. 156.
35. Jose Rawlins, pp. 16 and 18.
36. Interview with Harry Griffith Jenkins, 5 August 2006.

3 The Cardiff Pals

1. Quoted in Wikipedia article 'The Pals Battalions'.
2. K. Cooper and J. Davies, *The Cardiff Pals*, p. 12.
3. *South Wales Echo*, 8 October 1914.
4. *Ibid.*
5. *South Wales Echo*, 22 October 1914.
6. K. Cooper and J. Davies, p. 21.
7. *Ibid.*, p. 36.
8. *Ibid.*, p. 69.
9. The Cardiff Pals website.
10. Quoted in Jonathan Hicks, p. 25.
11. *Western Mail*, 5 January 1915.
12. *Western Mail*, 12 January 1915.
13. Dennis Morgan, *The Story of Cardiff*, p. 215.
14. *Western Mail*, 29 November 1915.
15. William Joshua, quoted on the Cardiff Pals website.

4 Three Ports

1. Dennis Morgan, p. 215.
2. John Richards, p. 106.
3. John Jibbs, *The Morels of Cardiff*, p. 107.
4. Trade Review of South Wales and Monmouthshire for 1914, 1 January 1915.
5. Julian Thompson, *The War at Sea, 1914–1918*, p. 192.
6. *Western Mail*, 15 March 1915.
7. John Richards, pp. 111 and 114.
8. Brian Lee, *Tiger Bay and the Docks*.
9. *South Wales Echo*, 24 July 1916.
10. *Penarth Advertiser*, 2 February 1915.
11. *South Wales Echo*, 26 July 1916.
12. *Ibid.*
13. *South Wales Echo*, 28 July 1916.
14. *South Wales Echo*, 5 August 1914.
15. Roy Thorne, *Penarth: A History*, p. 18.
16. *Penarth Times*, 27 August 1914.
17. Phil Carradice, *A Town in Conflict*, p. 38.
18. *Ibid.*, p. 45.
19. *Ibid.*, p. 52.
20. *Ibid.*, p. 5.
21. *Penarth Times*, 12 July 1917.
22. *Ibid.*, 11 January 1917, p. 7.
23. *Ibid.*
24. Interview with Ronnie Phillips, August 1969.
25. Jonathan Hicks, pp. 42–43.
26. *Penarth Advertiser*, 8 June 1915.
27. Quoted in Jonathan Hicks, p. 75.
28. *Barry Dock News*, 1 February 1918.
29. *Ibid.*, 11 October 1918.
30. *Ibid.*, 25 January 1918.
31. Conversation with Florence Evans, August 1991.

5 A Pier at War

1. *Ibid.*
2. *Penarth Times*, 19 August 1917.
3. *Penarth Times*, 26 April 1917.
4. *The Penarth News*, 7 December 1922.
5. Interview with Florence Evans, August 1991.
6. Quoted in Phil Carradice, *Penarth Pier*, p. 42.
7. *South Wales Echo*, 3 December 1914.
8. Nigel Coombes, *Passenger Steamers of the Bristol Channel*, pp. 50–51.

9. Phil Carradice, *Penarth Pier*, p. 39.
10. Lucinda Gosling, *Brushes and Bayonets*, p. 28.

6 Vale Soldiers at War

1. Wyn Griffiths, *Up to Mametz and Beyond*, p. 62.
2. *Penarth Advertiser*, 8 September 1914.
3. *South Wales Echo*, 29 December 1914.
4. Wyn Griffiths, pp. 14–15.
5. Frank Pope, quoted in Phil Carradice, *A Town at War*, p. 35.
6. Percy Thomas, quoted in Jonathan Hicks, p. 30.
7. *Western Mail*, 16 March 1915.
8. *Ibid.*, 1 January 1915.
9. Gunner Daniel Harries, quoted in Jonathan Hicks, p. 41.
10. Jose Rawlins, p. 19.
11. *South Wales Echo*, 3 May 1916.
12. *South Wales Echo*, 22 August 1914.
13. A. T. Rixon in *Penarth Times*, 26 August 1915.
14. Ivor Morgan quoted in *Voices of the First World War*.
15. *Penarth Times*, 4 January 1917.
16. Private C. Maunder in *Penarth Times*, 7 February 1916.
17. Sgt H. Marshman in *Barry Dock News*, 19 April 1918.
18. Diary of Sgt Jack Spear.
19. *Ibid.*
20. *Penarth Times*, 21 September 1916.
21. First World War Lives website.

7 Heroes and Villains, Vale Personalities at War

1. *Cardiff Times*, 5 July 1952.
2. Tony Williams in *Southerndown Golf Club*, p. 85.
3. *Penarth Times*, 11 January 1917.
4. Quoted in Jonathan Hicks, p. 114.
5. Phil Carradice, *A Town in Conflict*, pp. 61–2.
6. *South Wales Echo*, 13 July 1916.
7. Simon Gibbs, unpublished paper.
8. Phil Carradice, *First World War in the Air*, p. 11.
9. *South Wales Echo*, 10 November 1914.
10. *Ibid.*, 4 November 1914.
11. *Ibid.*
12. Phil Carradice, *A Town in Conflict*, p. 33.
13. Quoted in Jonathan Hicks, p. 94.
14. *South Wales Echo*, 6 May 1916.
15. *Western Mail*, 8 January 1915.

16. *South Wales Echo*, 9 May 1916.
17. *Ibid.*, 19 June 1916.
18. *Cardiff Times*, 26 July 1952.
19. *South Wales Echo*, 3 July 1918.
20. *Penarth Advertiser*, 2 November 1915.

8 War on the Home Front

1. Quoted in Jonathan Hicks, p. 8.
2. From *Penarth Times*, quoted in Phil Carradice, *A Town at War*, p. 39.
3. *Cardiff Times*, 12 July 1952.
4. Lucinda Gosling, p. 78.
5. *South Wales Echo*, 4 July 1916.
6. *Western Mail*, 16 November 1915.
7. Jonathan Hicks, p. 242.
8. Dennis Morgan, pp. 218–19.
9. *South Wales Echo*, 9 May 1916.
10. Dennis Morgan, p. 216–17.
11. *Barry Dock News*, 18 January 1918.
12. *Penarth Times*, 21 February 1918.
13. *Ibid.*, 22 February 1917.
14. *Barry Dock News*, 18 January 1918.
15. Interview with Harry Griffith Jenkins, 5 August 2006.
16. Interview with Ernest Plumb, September 2006.
17. Interview with Megan Rees, September 2006.
18. Interview with Alice Josephine Richards, September 2006.
19. Interview with Harry Griffith Jenkins, 5 August 2006.
20. Robert John Robertson, quoted in article by Alun Robertson in *Front Line*.

9 The End of the War

1. *South Wales Echo*, 31 July 1918.
2. Phil Carradice, *A Town in Conflict*, p. 53.
3. Lucinda Gosling, p. 174.
4. *Barry Dock News*, October 1916.
5. *Cardiff Times*, 2 August 1952.
6. Interview with Harry Griffith Jenkins, 5 August 2006.
7. Interview with Augusta Clubb, 13 June 2005.
8. *Barry Dock News*, 22 November 1924.
9. Penarth News, 13 November 1924.
10. Jose Rawlins, p. 45–6.
11. Dennis Morgan, p. 221.

Bibliography

Primary Sources

Interviews
(Copies held by author)

Augusta Clubb
Florence Evans
Harry Griffith Jenkins
Ronnie Phillips
Ernest Plumb
Megan Rees
Alice Josephine Richards

Diaries

Sgt Jack Spear (Penarth, RGA)
Thomas Henry Thomas (Rhondda)

Newspapers

Barry Dock News
Barry Herald
Cardiff Times
Penarth Advertiser
Penarth News
Penarth Times
South Wales Echo
Western Mail

Secondary Sources

Websites

BBC Wales History Blog
Cardiff Pals website
First World War Lives website
Wikipedia

Books

Anon. (ed.), *Front Line* (Cwm Press, for the Western Front Association, Cardiff, 1996)
Carradice, Phil, *Penarth Pier* (Baron, Northampton, 1994)
Carradice, Phil, *Penarth: The Story* (Penarth Press, Penarth 2004)
Carradice, Phil, *Southerndown Golf Club* (editor) (Private printing, Southerndown, 2005)
Carradice, Phil, *A Town in Conflict* (Penarth Press, Penarth, 2006)
Carradice, Phil, *People's Poetry of World War One* (Cecil Woolf, London, 2007)
Carradice, Phil, *The Great War, An Illustrated History* (Amberley, Stroud, 2010)
Carradice, Phil, *First World War in the Air* (Amberley, Stroud, 2012)
Coombes, Nigel, *Passenger Steamers of the Bristol Channel* (Twelveheads Press, Cornwall, 1990)
Cooper, K. and J. Davies, *The Cardiff Pals* (Militaria Cymraeg, Cardiff, 1998)
Gibbs, John, *Morels of Cardiff* (National Museum of Wales, Cardiff, 1982)
Gibbs, Simon, *John Angel Gibbs* (Unpublished paper, 2013)
Griffiths, Wyn, *Up to Mametz and Beyond* (Pen and Sword, Barnsley, 2012)
Hicks, Jonathan, *Barry and the Great War* (Fielding Publishing, Barry, 2007)
Hutton, John, *An Illustrated History of Cardiff Docks* (Silver Link, Kettering, 2009)
Donald Moore (ed.) *Barry: The Centenary Book* (Private printing, Barry, 1984)
Morgan, Dennis, *The Cardiff Story* (D. Brown and Sons, Cowbridge, 1991)
North, Geoffrey, *Barry* (Nonsuch Publications, Stroud, 1996)
Richards, John, *Cardiff: A Maritime History* (Tempus, Stroud, 2011)
Rawlins, Jose, *The Great War: Memorials of Cowbridge and Llanblethian* (Cowbridge Records Society, Cowbridge, 2008)
Thompson, Julian, *The War at Sea, 1914–1918* (Pan/Imperial War Museum, London, 2005)
Thorne, Roy, *Penarth: A History* (Starling Press, Newport, 1976)
Walklate, Neil, *A Step Back: St Nicholas* (Y Lolfa, Talybont, 2012)